LEARNING TRANSPORTED

Augmented, Virtual and Mixed Reality for All Classrooms

JAIME DONALLY

International Society for Technology in Education

PORTLAND, OREGON • ARLINGTON, VIRGINIA

Learning Transported
Augmented, Virtual and Mixed Reality for All Classrooms
Jaime Donally

© 2018 International Society for Technology in Education

Acquisitions Editor: *Valerie Witte*

Editor: *Emily Reed*

Copy Editor: *JV Bolkan*

Book Design and Production: *Jeff Puda*

Cover Design: *Edwin Ouellette*

Library of Congress Cataloging-in-Publication Data

Names: Donally, Jaime, author.

Title: Learning transported : augmented, virtual and mixed reality for all classrooms / Jaime Donally.

Description: Portland, Oregon : International Society for Technology in Education, [2018] | Includes bibliographical references and index.

Identifiers: LCCN 2017057021 (print) | LCCN 2018002127 (ebook) | ISBN 9781564846624 (mobi) | ISBN 9781564846631 (epub) | ISBN 9781564846648 (pdf) | ISBN 9781564843999 (pbk.)

Subjects: LCSH: Educational technology. | Virtual reality in education. | Education–Effect of technological innovations on.

Classification: LCC LB1028.3 (ebook) | LCC LB1028.3 .D62 2018 (print) | DDC 371.33--dc23

LC record available at https://lccn.loc.gov/2017057021

First Edition

ISBN: 978-1-56484-399-9

Ebook version available.

Printed in the United States of America

ISTE® is a registered trademark of the International Society for Technology in Education.

About ISTE

The International Society for Technology in Education (ISTE) is the premier non-profit organization serving educators and education leaders committed to empowering connected learners in a connected world. ISTE serves more than 100,000 education stakeholders throughout the world.

ISTE's innovative offerings include the ISTE Conference & Expo, one of the biggest, most comprehensive edtech events in the world—as well as the widely adopted ISTE Standards for learning, teaching and leading in the digital age and a robust suite of professional learning resources, including webinars, online courses, consulting services for schools and districts, books, and peer-reviewed journals and publications. Visit iste.org to learn more.

JOIN OUR COMMUNITY OF PASSIONATE EDUCATORS

ISTE members get free year-round professional development opportunities and discounts on ISTE resources and conference registration. Membership also connects you to a network of educators who can instantly help with advice and best practices.

Join or renew your ISTE membership today! Visit iste.org/membership or call 800.336.5191.

RELATED ISTE TITLES

Mobile Learning Mindset Series, by Carl Hooker

Gamify Literacy: Boost Collaboration, Comprehension and Learning, edited by Michele Haiken

To see all titles available from ISTE, please visit iste.org/resources.

About the Author

Jaime Donally is a passionate technology enthusiast. She began her career as a classroom teacher and later moved into instructional technology, where she invested in educators in her district. Her desire to build genuine relationships led to a forward-thinking PLN that embraces risk and innovation. She has started global events that have produced collaboration with educators and classrooms around the world.

Donally provides staff development and training on trending technology topics to conferences and districts around the country. Her latest adventures include the startup of Global Maker Day and the Hoonuit Learning Ambassador Program.

As her passion for immersive technology increases, her devotion to highlighting new classroom resources sparked the idea to create the #ARVRinEDU hashtag and weekly Twitter chat. In addition, she facilitates a discussion of immersive technology in Voxer on to support and share classroom discovery. While intrigued by the latest gadgets, her true passion is sharing resources that can be used with the tools we have available today.

Acknowledgments

I would like to acknowledge the many people who cheered me on to complete this work and share my passion for immersive technology with fellow educators. I am particularly grateful to my family for supporting me to persevere through the busiest of times.

To my husband Frank, who will share the joys of authorship with me soon, I can't thank you enough for pushing me to do great things. Even though you have no idea what I'm talking about, you listen to my ideas and lovingly grin, knowing that I speak "edtech" and you speak "Greek."

To my children, Elias, Hannah, and Elliana, who join me with excitement to test out every new toy and gadget. I couldn't do this work without my little tech geniuses.

To my mom, Linda, who has always believed in me. You've seen in me what I have never seen in myself and it's because of your faith that I learned to never give up.

To my Papi, who has been the best "manager" anyone could ever have.

Thanks to my amazing #ARVRinEDU PLN, especially to Marialice Curran, Andi McNair, and Rachelle Dene Poth, for supporting me on this journey.

I'm not qualified, nor did I have the confidence to complete this journey alone. It was through the grace of God that I had the opportunity to finish what He started.

I dedicate this book to all educators who take the leap into immersive technologies for the benefit of their students.

Contents

CHAPTER 8

Storytelling

CHAPTER 9

Preparing for the Future of Mixed Reality

Foreword

By BRAD WAID

U sing immersive technology in education is kind of like a rainbow. We know at the end of the rainbow there is an incredible reward, but sometimes we don't know where to begin. Jaime Donally gives us an excellent place to begin with her helpful guide to incorporating this amazing technology and leveraging it in a learning environment.

Augmented reality has been around for over twenty years in industry, but most technologies take time to make their way into education, and AR is no exception. One thing that has slowed it down is that it's not something physical, like a whiteboard or a set of new textbooks. It's more of an idea, a new way to look at learning and teaching.

AR allows you to bring learning experiences into the classroom that were never before possible. It allows you to place the solar system on a student's desk and bring the NASA Mars Rover to life. Virtual reality allows you to travel to places around the world through immersive experiences and even travel to the past and learn how to joust. And then there is mixed reality, which is similar to AR but allows the learning to interact with your surrounding environment, such as your classroom walls or a student's desk.

Jaime Donally has been on the leading edge of incorporating immersive technology in learning experiences since it first made its way into education and she has been a champion for many teachers and kids along the way. What she has been talking about, evangelizing, and presenting for years she has now put into one incredible well-written book.

Learning Transported is a comprehensive guide for everything thing you have wanted to know about immersive technology and a step-by-step manual to help you get started. It comes complete with great explanations, a glossary with definitions for the different technologies, classroom examples, recommended apps and tools, and sample lesson plans to get you started. It also addresses practical things like classroom space, cost, student benefit, and professional development.

Learning Transported is a can't miss for any teacher, administrator, or district interested in incorporating the latest emerging technologies into their classroom, building, or district.

BRAD WAID is an award-winning educator, emerging technology leader, global influencer, and international keynote speaker in both education and industry. Recognized as the #14 global influencer in augmented reality, he is also a blogger, writer, visionary, and futurist and was awarded by the National School Board Association as one of the "20 to Watch" in 2013. He is the COO and Director of Emerging Technologies for The Digital Citizenship Institute and the author of the upcoming book *Digital Overlap*.

Introduction

How many students come home after school sharing that they walked around the solar system during class? How often do our students have the opportunity to create 3D worlds or hold holograms in their hands? The chances are unlikely that many students get to engage in these types of learning activities, however, with the technology flooding to the public, we're beginning to see more of these experiences adapted for the classroom and popping up in lesson plans.

Many educators think the only way for students to have these kinds of experiences is through an expensive technology purchase or by having a technology expert bring it together. The truth is that many resources are available now on the devices that are already in the classroom. The implementation of these tools can be as simple as opening an app or loading a website. Although the media is hyping the latest gadgets that can carry enormous costs, companies are creating tools that meet the same educational needs for free or at a fraction of the price.

The goal of this book is to show you the possibilities for bringing immersive technologies to your students. While the field is new and the technology constantly changing, we can begin to see the potential these tools have for creating uniquely engaging learning experiences. While exploring the many resources available for students, you'll find recommendations to provide the most successful implementation. As districts are beginning to make decisions, you'll also get purchase suggestions from the classroom, curriculum, and technology perspective. Having access to a full picture and a realistic plan of action when making these purchases will make every dollar count and ensure a greater chance for success.

Using This Book

The first part of this book defines and describes immersive technology in the context of education. For those unfamiliar with the term, immersive technology refers to "technology that blurs the line between the physical world and digital or simulated world, thereby creating a sense of immersion" (Wikipedia, 2017). For the purposes of this book, immersive technology refers to virtual, augmented, and mixed reality. Many of us first heard about virtual reality in the '90s, when movies like *Lawnmower Man* and *The Matrix* painted pictures of computer-generated worlds we could access through complicated hardware. The direction virtual reality has taken is decidedly different and no longer available to only a select few. Augmented reality, too, has grown from QR codes to experiences that add interactive layers to our everyday surroundings; think Pokemon Go! Mixed reality, an experience that combines elements of virtual and mixed reality, brings virtual objects to the real world, where we can engage with them in lifelike simulations. Readers will become familiar with these terms and what types of experiences characterize them.

Successful implementation depends upon careful research and planning. Chapters three and four address what to consider before bringing immersive technology to the classroom, including which device to choose and how space, infrastructure, and training should be factored into planning.

When you are ready to take the plunge, the next three chapters will get your feet wet exploring a variety of augmented, virtual, and mixed reality tools. Chapter 5 takes you through the process of sharing immersive technology with your students in the form of six full lesson plans. Designed for use with existing technology, these lessons address different content areas and are mapped to standards. Chapter 6 invites you to get inspired by trying out several tools as part of learning activities with your students. Find out how to plan a virtual field trip or scavenger hunt. Today's students are eager creators, not just consumers, of content. Find out how to design and customize your experiences in Chapter 7. For a look to the future, Chapter 8 explores the unique ways that immersive technology is shaping storytelling and Chapter 9 shares some of the newest technologies coming to mixed reality.

For help navigating the myriad of tools and terms, the book includes a glossary and appendix of apps.

Experiencing This Book

Enjoy interactive features in the book that provide links to content, 3D objects, and videos. When you need additional support, or want to engage further in the material, these interactive features provide an immersive experience to deepen your understanding. You can access the directions on how to engage in the book on my website at **arvrinedu.com**.

Another way to interact with the book is by participating in activities. At the end of every chapter, you can take the Learning Transported Challenge. These challenges will give you the chance to put into practice the suggestions and concepts from the book. When you complete the challenge, you can share what you've created with other educators on social media using the hashtag #ARVRinEDU. Each challenge will include beginner and intermediate options to provide flexibility and opportunity for growth. The challenges can give you the practice and support to successfully use immersive technology with your students.

1 Understanding Augmented, Virtual, and Mixed Reality

When was the last time you took a trip to the moon and explored the craters on the surface? What! You've never traveled to the moon? You don't need to wait to book a private trip to your dream locations anymore with access to immersive technology tools. We can now provide our students the opportunity to experience what we've read about in printed textbooks for several decades. If a picture is worth a thousand words, then why not give them a million more?

The terms augmented and virtual reality are often interchanged in the education community. Many times, because of the lack of knowledge between the two technologies, the terms are connected to mean the same thing or interchanged by mistake. This chapter distinguishes the differences between augmented and virtual reality, introduces mixed reality, and describes how all three are used within the context of the classroom.

Augmented Reality

Augmented reality (AR) refers to an enhanced version of reality afforded by the use of technology that overlays digital information on an image of something being viewed through a device (Merriam-Webster.com, n.d.). What does that mean? The view through a device camera includes a digital layer on top. The digital layer gives the illusion that we see something in our physical world that's not really there. An example of AR in a classroom is viewing a digital version of a beating heart that's sitting on a physical desk. Although it's unlikely to see a beating heart outside of the body, augmented reality makes it possible by providing a digital layer that is viewed in 3D. You can bring this technology into your lessons by using many of the devices we already have in the classroom. Most AR is best viewed through a mobile device such as a smartphone or tablet. Augmented reality uses the device's camera, GPS, and gyroscope to create the experience.

Trigger Images

Augmented reality often uses a trigger image or target to activate the digital layer. The trigger is similar to the concept of a bar code or QR code. When scanning a barcode, the computer knows what action to take or what information to locate. When your device identifies a trigger image or target, it knows what digital information to populate and where to place it. In most instances, trigger images cause a device to populate a 3D object, image, or video that can be seen through the screen of the device.

When scanning trigger images, lighting is important. Barcodes are scanned by devices at store checkouts and other places to identify information about the product labeled with the code. The codes are easy to scan because they are high-contrast images—typically black print on top of a white background. Unlike barcodes, trigger images are often full color images instead of lines and bars.

Try It! Scanning a Trigger Image

If you'd like to experience augmented reality, you can view the trigger image in Figure 1.1 using the Spacecraft 3D app by Nasa. Find the iOS app at **tiny.cc/spacecraftapple** and the Android app at **tiny.cc/spacecraftandroid**.

AR Target for SPACECRAFT 3D
Jet Propulsion Laboratory/California Institute of Technology

Photo: NASA/JPL-Caltech/Malin Space Science Systems

Figure 1.1

The Spacecraft 3D app by Nasa Jet Propulsion allows you to scan trigger images such as this to learn more about the Earth and other planets.

The contrast between the colors is also important for the device to locate the exact trigger image. Lighting can make all the colors look darker or lighter, which can diminish the contrast. One of the biggest problems with lighting and contrast when scanning trigger images comes from the glare in books or printed images. Finding the best lighting will begin with trial and error, but you quickly learn what works best.

GPS

When a trigger image isn't required for AR, the device will populate a digital image that is floating on top of your camera. An example of this technology is in the Pokémon Go app. While you look around through your camera on your device, you'll see a layer of an object on top of your view. The 2D or 3D object is placed in the correct spot using the GPS location of the device. The many apps that use your location with AR can be used in scavenger hunts, quests, gaming, messaging, social media, and much more.

Gyroscope

A gyroscope determines where to place the overlaid object in AR and has become a standard feature on many mobile devices. The gyroscope is not the same thing as GPS. Augmented reality apps use the gyroscope to sense the rotations of the device and determine what motions you make. When you spin around, look up, or look down, the gyroscope in your device is making it possible to place objects in specific spots for the best AR experience.

In short, augmented reality is magic, or at least that's what your students will think. You have access to technology that provides illusions with layered objects through the camera view. Do you want to bring the solar system into your classroom? Check! Do you want to bring books to life by scanning the pages? Check! Do you want to pull a bunny out of a hat? I don't see the academic benefit, but sure, check!

Virtual Reality

Moving on to virtual reality (VR), we see some of the same technology being used, such as trigger images, GPS, and the gyroscope. These technologies provide the opportunity to view a digital experience without using your device camera. We are no longer looking at our reality through our camera with a new experience layered on top, but fully immersed into a digital experience that replaces our reality.

The definition of virtual reality is "an artificial environment that is experienced through sensory stimuli (such as sights and sounds) provided by a computer and in which one's actions partially determine what happens in the environment (Merriam-Webster.com, n.d.)." Classroom teachers have traditionally been limited to the experiences they are able to give to a student, but VR has broken these barriers.

The technology uses a completely digital experience to surround you in a "false environment." The environment can be digitally created or it can be a video from an actual experience. The view through your device is wrapped around you in 360°. You can look up, down, left, and right to see the scene. The VR experience gives you the illusion that you're standing in the center of a particular space.

Virtual reality can be as simple as images and video. Multiple images can be taken from every point of view and stitched together to make a sphere of pictures. Viewed through the center of the sphere, you have the illusion that you're located at that same place, although you're really looking at multiple images that have been seamlessly pieced together.

A benefit of VR experiences is the flexibility to view them on multiple platforms. Because augmented reality uses the device camera to bring experiences to life, Chromebooks or laptops with their semi-stationary cameras are limited in AR features. Using virtual reality, however, you can click, drag around, and view spherical photos from a computer. Keep in mind, the experience isn't as impressive on a computer as it is in a viewer or on a mobile device.

When determining the difference between augmented and virtual reality, people tend to confuse the two terms. The difference between augmented and virtual reality is easily identified by whether the experience uses the device camera or not. When using AR, the camera combines a real and digital view, whereas VR is purely digital. These differences are easy to distinguish when given the definition, but the next term in immersive technology is more difficult to identify: mixed reality.

Mixed Reality

Mixed or merged reality (MR) looks very similar to augmented reality in that the view is a digital layer through your camera. Many mixed reality tools are able to link digital objects to real-world objects while using our natural gestures to interact with the content.

Mixed reality combines digital interaction with the experience of the real world. In doing so, MR takes augmented reality experiences to the next level by allowing our real and digital worlds to interact with one another. Instead of seeing a only digital layer on top our real world, we now see information that identifies and interacts with our physical environment, such as walls and furniture. For example, using only AR, a digital layer portraying a three-dimensional skull might float on top of your camera view. When the skull is made in mixed reality, the digital layer can allow the skull to sit on your table to give a much more realistic interaction. These digital objects can actually run behind furniture and break through walls.

The mixed reality experience can even allow you to manipulate objects using your fingers. You no longer need a mouse to click and drag around in the 2D space, but can pinch, select, and drag objects all around your classroom. I see mixed reality as the next level of immersive technology because it interacts with our real world. The MR technology is more relevant to real situations, which makes the adjustment to the technology less abstract.

Wide-scale classroom implementation of immersive technologies such as AR, VR, and MR will be more likely once they are available for standard classroom equipment. Although these technologies are currently being developed on high-end devices, the technology is rapidly becoming more commonly available and inexpensive. The development of mobile apps and computer tools continues to grow, especially in the education sector.

Learning Transported Challenge

What are the differences between AR, VR, and MR and how has your understanding of them changed based on what you read in this chapter?

Using what you've learned, create a Venn diagram to identify the similarities and differences in augmented, virtual, and mixed reality. Include text and visual examples to support your reasoning. For an advanced challenge, design a digital graphic that defines the difference between AR, VR, and MR. Include resources and examples to justify your answer.

Brainstorm ways that each of the three immersive technologies introduced in this chapter might be used: in the future workforce, in education, and in your classroom. Share with your colleagues or your students.

2 Why Use AR, VR, and MR in Education?

When sharing immersive technology with educators, I rarely find a bored audience. Educators are eager to dive into the technology and are awestruck with the incredible power of these resources. We giggle, squeal, and even gasp as these tools are unveiled with examples of amazing new experiences to be had. I assumed teachers would use AR, VR, and MR immediately; I was surprised when I found they weren't.

I discovered that although many educators were won over by the wow factor, they couldn't see a direct connection between immersive technology tools and content areas and student objectives. I had to face the reason why teachers were struggling to adapt these tools to the classroom. Although the experience was fun and engaging, the application needed to be clearly laid out with a direct connection to student standards and lesson plans.

To establish the legitimacy of immersive technology, this chapter addresses the reason these tools should be welcomed into the classroom. We'll begin with the most important reason, student benefit, then address changes happening in the classroom and finally, look at standards.

Student Benefit

One of the most obvious benefits of immersive technology is piquing the students' interest. Most students want to explore learning through a technology lens and these tools are still building momentum, making this the prime time to capture their attention. Students are eager to see the new technology because it's part of their culture. Technology is embedded into our everyday lives, and it's even more important for our students and their future work and social lives. There is quite a lot of attention to and discussion of immersive technologies in the media and your students are undoubtedly curious. They have probably encountered immersive technology in some shape or form already, through games or other entertainment. Seeing it figure into a lesson or curricular activity will likely cause them to be intrigued and engaged in the content.

In addition to increased student engagement, there are a number of ways immersive technology can benefit student learning, including:

- Providing authentic learning experiences.
- Transporting students to places outside of the classroom.
- Offering support and a means of communication for ELL students.
- Creating innovative spaces to collaborate and share information.

Authentic Learning

Research is showing that immersive technologies provide improvement in knowledge retention. In a study done by Juan, Mendez-Lopez, Perez-Hernandez, and Albiol-Perez, learners showed an increase in memory improvement in pre- and post-test results when using augmented reality in the lesson (2014). When the learning is authentic, we have an opportunity to engage students with purposeful, deepened learning.

Going Beyond the Walls of the Classroom

We are finding more of schools limiting field trips and outings due to many factors, yet at the same time we face an increased demand for improved student performance. For example, our students are expected to know about the ocean. They need to read and write about the ocean. They're expected to identify marine species and describe the relationship of ocean tides to marine life. Yet, how many of our students have never been to the ocean? Using immersive technology tools, you can eliminate the limitations of location or funding and take your students on virtual field trips to places like the Great Barrier Reef.

The limits we have in our real world are no longer limitations in our classrooms. A student can explore places that have never been an option in the past, and it's because of this incredible technology that the learning can be realistic. According to researchers Mehmet & Yasin,

"This new approach enhances the effectiveness and attractiveness of teaching and learning. The ability to overlay computer generated virtual things onto the real world changes the way we interact, and trainings become real that can be seen in real time rather than a static experience." (Mehmet & Yasin, 2012)

Communication

As we face budgetary and logistical issues in our classrooms, our students also face challenges that hinder learning. One obstacle that some students face is a language barrier. When English language learners have access to immersive technology, they're no longer hindered by understanding, because the experience speaks for itself. Companies are beginning to create tools that use the benefits of immersive technology to support communication. Our students can experience learning no matter their level of language proficiency, and we can build on the needed vocabulary without losing the opportunity for knowledge acquisition in the process.

Collaboration

Students can use immersive technology to access resources. Although we may not always have face-to-face access to an expert or tutor, we now have access to virtual support that can describe, share, and demonstrate the knowledge our students need for deeper understanding and real-world application. Moving beyond online videos, our students can access more realistic and effective support in AR, VR, and MR.

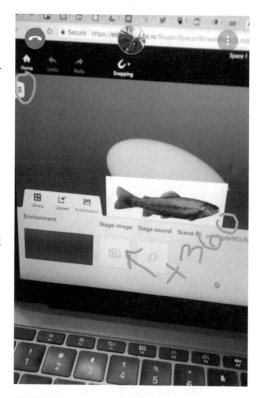

One example of this is a mobile app called Vuforia Chalk, which uses video chats layered with augmented reality to collaborate in real-time. Users share a live view of what they are looking at and, through the chat window, they are able to add and see eachother's annotations. The website for the app (**chalk. vuforia.com**) uses the example of a mother explaining to her son how to use the washing machine. During their chat, both draw circles and arrows to identify different controls on

Figure 2.1

Vuforia Chalk augmented reality chat app.

the washing machine. Gone is the frustration of trying to explain something without being able to see what the other person is looking at.

An example of using Vuforia Chalk in the classroom could be a global collaboration with another class that describes how to play a musical instrument, or a student project where a new program is being used. Figure 2.1 shows how to support someone using the CoSpaces app on their computer by showing them where to add a 360 image to change the environment. The Vuforia Chalk app is currently available in the iOS App Store at **tiny.cc/chalkapp**. Try it the next time you need to demonstrate a new tool or walk someone through a procedure.

Viewed through the lens of education, these tools can help illustrate real-world problems and allow students to collaborate on creative ways to solve them. Immersive technology is an open door for our students young and old to develop the skills to create the future of entertainment, education, and productivity.

Transformed Classrooms

Although some of our classrooms are still set up the same way they looked decades ago, others have evolved into interactive spaces. Likewise, teaching methods are also evolving. Our classrooms look different but, more importantly, our students engage in learning differently. Memorizing is no longer the emphasis and the "sit and get" motto is long overdue for retirement.

Our classrooms and teaching methods are evolving because we are constantly adapting to the needs of our students. We're searching for tools that adapt to individual preferences and customizing the experience based on the needs of the individual student. Immersive technology offers powerful tools that we can harness to provide these personalized and custom learning experiences.

Although it's sadly true that the pace of change can be slow, especially in the education environment, the good news is that solutions are coming from two directions. As noted earlier, software and applications are rapidly being adopted from the high-end systems into the technology levels common in schools and, at the same time, the power of those affordable classroom technologies is increasing to be able to deliver better experiences.

Already, many schools provide students with technology well-suited for immersive reality. Additionally, school networks are becoming more robust and powerful. This evolution will continue and, soon, every student in every classroom will have the resources to participate in VR. A good educator identifies the interests of their students and meshes them with learning activities in the classroom. Recently, we witnessed the incredible popularity of Pokémon Go, which attracted users through augmented reality, gamification, and competition. Combining the excitement of playing an AR game (identifying your students' interests) with your lesson objectives is the start to having the most success with immersive technology.

Knowing our students is the first step in developing the best plan in using immersive technology. In a recent interview with Dr. Richard Webb, head of the Innovative Design Studio at the University of Alaska, Anchorage, he indicated our students use a part of their brain when playing that goes beyond their subconscious and into a deeper level of learning. This knowledge allows students to learn faster and retain that knowledge longer and it's something that we're only beginning to understand. Watch my full interview with Dr. Webb at **tiny.cc/webbinterview**.

Some of the fears that seem to haunt educators when learning to adapt immersive technology to classroom needs is that students will always expect fun instead of practical learning. In most cases, if we had a problem with students having too much fun at school, wouldn't we also not face the challenge of student dropout, behavioral problems, and lack of attention? Our issue with fun in the classroom is a result of our own issue to adapt to our students' needs for their greatest opportunity for success.

Some of the visual changes we'll begin to see more of in our classrooms surround access to power. The quantity of devices is growing and becoming more individualized. The standard computer lab is becoming more flexible and mobile to transition from class to class. In addition to power, we also see an adjustment to access points. Having a strong signal in all parts of the school where learning happens, including libraries and open spaces, is critical for the best possible experiences.

How our students interact with content is also transforming. Our students no longer look at textbooks the same way. They expect that lessons will and should include interactive activities. Textbook publishers are already jumping on board and delivering dynamic lesson activities that include augmented, virtual, and mixed reality experiences.

Imagine opening a textbook to the topic of storms and seeing a picture of a tornado. Now compare that to the experience of hearing the tornado winds whipping around you, from the left and right, and turning around to see a truck trailer being thrown onto the road. These experiences provide completely different interactions with a subject and open the door for different activities and discussions. It's important to find the right interactions to meet our student's needs.

Standards continue to demand the same type of knowledge such as reading and writing, but we now see an evolution toward experience and engagement. While reading a book, a student can scan the pages to see the imaginary characters come to life. Students can now write a story and layer characters on top of a drawing with augmented reality props. Imagine the stories our students will want to write when they know they can enhance the content using AR.

When we begin to see the possibilities immersive technology can offer, we start to see opportunities to bring experiences to our students that we can't always offer them in real life. You would never bring your students outside to experience a real tornado, but you might use a virtual reality tool to show how powerful the winds of an F5 tornado can be. Using immersive technology, you can bring your students to the eye of the tornado without putting them in any danger.

Discovery, Education, and Retention

The difference in going from 2D to 3D interactions is similar to seeing your favorite actress on television, then meeting her in person. The two are as different as night and day; one is the interaction we experience while the other is the impression we have from TV. Although we may think we know what something looks like, the truth is we only make an assumption until we see it in real life.

Studies are trying to keep up with immersive technology as it continues to take the spotlight. In the article "Immersive Tech in Education" on edtechtimes.com, author Charlie Scanlan recognizes that the future of immersive [technology] is uncertain, but the trend of mobile learning is growing and it may change education "as we know it" (Scanlan, 2017). We can easily see the difference in learning when students can bridge the connection between content in a book and real-life relevance. Bring that learning to the next phase by viewing 3D objects in the classroom and dissecting those objects to explore what is inside.

When given the opportunity, students want to discover learning themselves rather than being told the answer. Asking for someone to explain their experience when skydiving isn't a substitute for the experience you would have when skydiving yourself. When we steal the opportunity for our students to discover these experiences on their own, we prevent them from fully understanding the content and leave them repeating facts rather than knowing them. Reproducing information is not knowledge, but merely memorization.

If I asked what was the most powerful learning opportunity you remember in school, what lessons come to mind? It's likely those experiences included problem solving, engagement, and interaction. Those events were meaningful because they deepened your knowledge by allowing you to embrace the learning as your own. Personalized learning is a major benefit in immersive technology because the adventure changes in every session based on the individual's interest at that time. A student can watch 360° videos multiple times and have different encounters each time. These discoveries make the learning more meaningful and long lasting.

Opportunity and Empathy

Making individual connections to content and learning is a major focus of immersive technology, however, there are other benefits that support our society as a whole. We are finding that AR, VR, and MR allow students to shape how they view others around the world through interactions and collaboration. As students build social interactions with individuals through collaboration tools, they're learning about diversity and conditions outside of their location.

One of the problems our students face is being limited to their own geographic area, which can result in a limited worldview when it comes to different cultures, beliefs, and societies. As incredible as it would be to bring our students on a trip across the world, very rarely do we have that opportunity. Our worldview is shaped by our experiences, and because most of our students don't have the opportunity to travel outside of the country, we need to continue to find ways to help them experience and understand other lifestyles around the world.

A clear example of building global connections and developing empathy for others is the 360° video projects that show refugee camps and travel to third world countries that lack the basic resources that humans need to survive. This type of experience can be found on the YouVisit app under the topic, "Inside Syrian Lives" or by visiting **youvisit.com/rescue** from a computer. When our students are exposed to these situations, they must address how they feel about other people who face trials around the world. These experiences might never be possible without this technology.

Figure 2.2

Syrian Lives shares information in 360°.

Alignment with Standards

The ISTE Standards for Students address important skills that our students must possess to prepare them for opportunities and success in the future. The student standards capture different aspects of immersive technology that makes these resources so meaningful. Going through the standards and the connected indicators will show how to purposefully address student expectations and provide worthwhile learning. The full ISTE Standards for Students can be found in Appendix B. To learn more about the ISTE Standards and view the standards for educators, visit **iste.org/standards**.

Student Empowerment

The first standard focuses on student empowerment. In the process of using other technology in the classroom, students are building the skills needed to understand emerging technologies. For instance, when a student learns how to take photos, they are building foundational skills that will help them take 360° photos in the future. They will apply their troubleshooting knowledge from their past photography experiences toward the expectations of tomorrow. When we have the basic skills covered using our day-to-day activities, we are essentially giving our students the proficiency to be successful in future skills and potential careers.

Digital Citizenship

The next standard centers on our students as digital citizens. Managing your digital identity is a key skill in a world where global, virtual collaboration is becoming more and more common. Our students need to practice safe, legal, and ethical behavior in a 3D space just as they do in a 2D space. Issues such as intellectual property and copyright are the same within a virtual scene as they are in the real world. In addition, protecting their personal data is equally important when in a virtual environment as it is in a 2D environment. Students gain experience dealing with these concepts in the real world and in 2D environments. The deeper learning that immersive technologies can provide reinforces the importance of being a good digital citizen.

Student Creation

The third standard addresses students as knowledge constructors. Our students should be moving beyond passive experiences to designing and creating products that demonstrate their knowledge. The potential is endless when giving our students the baton to build classroom learning environments. Imagine a classroom where research is no longer restricted to a computer screen or textbook. Our students can collaborate with other students around the world to solve problems that they experience through the lens of a peer thousands of miles away. We don't need students to just be creators of content, but also to find ways to adapt their learning methods to find their greatest success in life.

Design and Innovation

The fourth standard is concentrated on innovative design using technology. Students develop creative solutions that provoke problem solving, experimentation, and idea discovery. We have the option for students to meet virtually in breakout areas outside of the classroom to work on projects, brainstorm, or even develop prototypes. We're no longer restricted by physical proximity and space constraints to allow collaboration or opportunities to connect to solve a problem—we can provide more options in a digital 3D environment.

Computational Thinking

The fifth standard looks to develop a classroom where students demonstrate their computational skills through a variety of technologies. Students use methods to identify, collect, and analyze data using algorithms. One valuable tool to support student connections with data is using virtual mind maps. Using tools such as

Bubbl.us and Canva, students can create a virtual mind map and visually display information in a 360° view.

Creative Communication

The sixth standard is focused on the student as a creative communicator. Students should use a variety of platforms to creatively and clearly communicate. Our classrooms are full of potential with immersive technology that can be used in visualizing information. In the use of virtual reality simulations, 3D models, and digital content, our students have the resources available to fully express and show their thoughts and ideas.

Global Collaboration

The last student standard is identifying the characteristics of the global collaborator. Students are expected to work with group and individual peers inside and outside of the classroom. Through virtual connections, students can experience life-like situations in other parts of the world to broaden their perspectives. Students can "travel" to other parts of the world to engage in discussions that expand their perspectives.

Learning Transported Challenge

What do you think the benefits are for students using immersive technology? Are you able to find any research supporting your claims? Share your findings in a blog post or post them to the community using the #ARVRinEDU hashtag.

Choose one of the ISTE Standards for Students (found in Appendix B) and explore ways that students might embody the standard through their use of augmented, virtual, or mixed reality.

3 Things to Consider Before You Get Started

As with most emerging technologies, there is a sense among many in education that the costs of entry are too high to make them justifiable for classroom implementation. It is easy to believe that the requirements in equipment are unfeasible and that the learning curve is too steep to be worth the effort. Often, these issues are emphasized by the very people urging adoption of the technology. It is always tempting to look at what is "just about possible" and get so excited that you overlook what is already possible and practical today.

We hear almost endless hype about new immersive technologies just coming on the market. Then we hear that the newest VR headset carries an unreasonably high price tag. Although the excitement over expensive, cutting-edge technology will continue, it is important to remember that educators can integrate these resources without breaking the budget or being a tech genius. As we go through the keys for successful implementation in this chapter, we will address how AR, VR, and MR can be used from a free or low-cost perspective for the average classroom.

Technical Knowledge

Most of the teachers I've talked to about implementing immersive technology in the classroom don't think they're tech savvy enough to provide such technology. They're wrong; they simply haven't been exposed to the accessibility and relatively easy learning curve of the available tools. Most resources are simple enough for even our youngest students to pick up and begin using with little instruction.

Immersive Technology Glossary

AUGMENTED REALITY (AR)

Trigger Image / Target / Marker - Images that cause a specific action to be performed by a device when viewed by the device's camera. This is similar to a barcode that, when scanned within a specific app, produces a description of the product associated with the barcode.

Overlays - The layer of content that is displayed on top of your camera view. The overlay items can vary from 2D images to 3D animated objects.

> *EXAMPLE* - Viewing an image of an insect (the trigger image) through the camera on a device displays an animated 3D insect. The overlay on top of the printed image gives the illusion that a bug is crawling around on your paper.

VIRTUAL REALITY (VR)

360° - This number represents a full spherical view that's layered all around the user.

Stitching - The term stitching is used to describe how multiple images or videos are layered next to each other and tied together to give the user the experience of being in that location.

Cardboard - An inexpensive VR viewer that's made of cardboard and designed to work with a smartphone. Often, the viewer includes controls to make selections on items the user sees in the experience.

Handheld Controller - Many Android devices allow the use of a Bluetooth connected controller. Many new headset technologies, particularly those designed for specific cell phone models, have their own controller.

Combined with the unfounded fear of the technology level required is an unfamiliarity with the various terms used. Gaining comfort with the terms and definitions used in immersive technology can cause most of these fears to dissipate. You can also experiment with the technology without first knowing all the lingo. The more experience you have using various platforms, the more comfortable you'll be moving forward and the easier it will be to conquer the vocabulary. Some of the terms to support you in implementing the tools are shared here in a glossary.

Directional Sound / Spatial Sound - Sounds become louder when you get closer and diminish when you are leaving a location, providing a more immersive and realistic experience.

EXAMPLE — You virtually experience an apple orchard by running an application on your smartphone that is coupled with a cardboard headset. You can see trees all around you, the ground below, and the sky above because the 360° image consists of many photos that have been stitched together. You may use your handheld controller to select a specific apple that could launch you into a marketplace where the chirping of birds is heard behind you. Each of directions you look could include a different sound file that gets louder or softer based on the direction you're looking.

MIXED REALITY (MR)

Gestures - A specific way to interact with content using our natural hand gestures.

Surface Tracking - Identify the space through the camera view such as floors, walls, and tables.

EXAMPLE — A virtual apple that appears to be sitting on a student's desk can be "picked up" and moved to the actual teacher's desk using gestures. The apple will appear to be sitting naturally on the teacher's desk because the application uses surface tracking to determine that the virtual apple is on a solid surface.

Another thing to be aware of when first starting out is the range of tools available. Resources for immersive technology vary from a teacher tool to a developer tool, so it's wise to know the landscape. The selection of the resources will determine the ease of use. Although basic application of the tools can be created and modified to be appropriate for students as young as preschool age, the complexity of the technology can be so high that only post-college developers would understand them. Understanding the different resources and their requirements will give you the freedom to select the tools that best meet your needs and skill level.

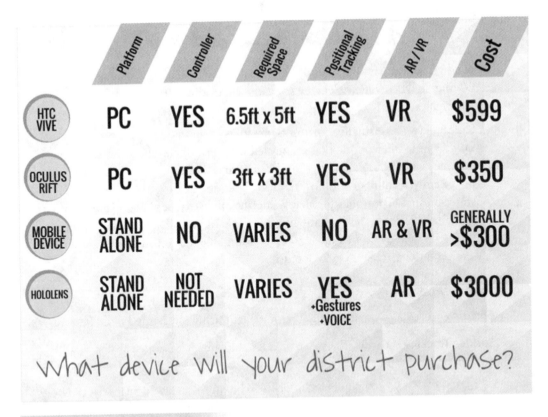

	Platform	Controller	Required Space	Positional Tracking	AR / VR	Cost
HTC VIVE	PC	YES	6.5ft x 5ft	YES	VR	$599
OCULUS RIFT	PC	YES	3ft x 3ft	YES	VR	$350
MOBILE DEVICE	STAND ALONE	NO	VARIES	NO	AR & VR	GENERALLY >$300
HOLOLENS	STAND ALONE	NOT NEEDED	VARIES	YES +Gestures +VOICE	AR	$3000

What device will your district purchase?

Figure 3.1
Select the Right Device

While prior knowledge of AR, VR, and MR is not required to start using immersive technology tools, it is recommended to have a basic knowledge of mobile devices and computer skills. Often a misconception, the use of immersive technology won't require more skill than using any other app or website.

Some of the basic skills needed are:

- Locating and downloading the specific apps onto a mobile device or computer.
- Setting up accounts within the various programs.
- Refreshing the page or restarting the app should you run into any glitches.

The tools in Appendix A include links to download them from iTunes or the Android store. You should practice downloading, opening, and using a tool before planning to bring it to the classroom.

Devices

Another false expectation of immersive technology is the idea that each student must have his or her own device. Many lessons are configured to work on central stations or by group work that would use only a handful of devices at a single time. Considering the various costs, requirements, and the variety of experiences, selecting the right device is key to beginning the immersive technology journey.

When evaluating the requirements for each device, the options are clear what would work best for a classroom setting. Although each of the devices listed in the chart in Figure 3.1 can provide an incredible experience, most of the devices were intended for private use. Considering the cost, space, training, and computer requirements, the mobile device is the most flexible to provide beneficial learning interactions in a classroom setting.

Infrastructure and Network Requirements

Choosing the right device is important, but an even more critical component is your classroom infrastructure. When using mobile devices, the need for Wi-Fi is top priority. Most immersive technology apps require a network connection to pull in the correct content. Although Wi-Fi may be available to your classroom, bandwidth will determine what content you can access and on how many devices it can effectively run.

There are times when you'll want all students actively participating on individual devices. These experiences typically work best in a computer lab where the devices are using a more robust, wired network. The use of a computer to click and drag around to look at a 360° view isn't quite as immersive as desired, but it can be a substitute when resources and bandwidth are limited.

If you have a high-quality Head-Mounted Display (HMD), you'll need a powerful computer to run the applications. Examples of using a computer to run the experience on a HMD are the HTC Vive and the Oculus Rift. Both of these systems display information in the HMD based on what the computer is sending over.

When beginning to implement immersive technology, districts most commonly ask which viewer they should purchase. Although the viewer plays a role in the experience, the device that's running the experience plays the most important role. The device can be a computer or a mobile device and the quality of that device can limit or enhance the immersive experience.

AR & VR in Browser

There are incredible options to use immersive technology from within the browser. This means you can explore immersive technology on almost any device that can connect to the internet. Browser-based AR and VR doesn't require the latest operating system or a specific app to download. The technology is built into the website's code so that when you open the website, your camera triggers an image or you are immediately pulled into a 360° experience. The enormous opportunity for using AR and VR in education grows significantly as many older devices can be useful tools for these experiences.

Depending on the website, the browser experience with AR and VR is fast and easy. The activities are engaging because multiple users can participate in the lesson at the same time. One site, called the Musical Forest (**forest.web-vrexperiments.com**) allows participants to enter a forest where they can click and drag to see a 360° view of their surroundings (Figure 3.2). The forest is filled with shapes that, when clicked, play a variety of sounds. A single user can "play" the shapes, or multiple users can enter the space and play instruments together. The activity is a great reminder that we may not be limited

Figure 3.2
The Musical Forest is one example of a VR experience on a browser.

by our device's age, operating system, or available space much longer as web based immersive technology is growing in popularity and capability.

Cost and Funding

Preparing for a new technology purchase requires research and a specific plan to make the best choice. Although basic VR viewers are quite inexpensive and generally work with a wide variety of mobile devices, choosing the devices (typically phones) is much more complex. When selecting the right mobile device, there are a few questions to keep in mind.

1. **Can the device handle the graphics and speed required for the experience to function?**

When faced with limited resources, some teachers have collected older phones to try to piece together a class set for augmented and virtual reality experiences. Cell phone technology has advanced rapidly over the past few years and immersive technology can expose the limitations of older phones. Most current smart phone models are sufficiently powerful to handle most AR and VR applications. Of course, more powerful phones with faster displays will deliver better experiences. Thinking ahead, one must also consider which devices will be more likely to be able to handle future applications that require more power.

2. **What are important features to consider in a new device purchase?**

Although it is difficult to predict future needs because immersive technology is growing at such an enormous rate, a basic rule of thumb is to consider devices in their first or second year of release. The key issue here is the device's operating system. Changes in operating systems often happen yearly, so the goal is to have a device that can last three to five new upgrades. Having a clear plan on your preferred device features may be limited to our current knowledge of technology available, but preparing for a four to five year window is the best way to get the most out of your purchasing budget.

When making a purchase, it's a great idea to consider the reputation of the device. An off-brand device is a risk when it hasn't established a history of reliability. Although the cost break may be enticing, replacements may be needed more often. Make your choice wisely and do your research. Check the web for device reviews and, if possible, reach out to your PLN or other educators to see if anyone has experience with the device. The ISTE communities are a great place to ask questions such as this.

3. **How much should I spend on a new device?**

The prices can range dramatically from older, off-brand devices to popular, newer devices. The device I typically recommend is the Apple iPad (Pro, 2017, or newer) for many reasons. The first benefit of the iPad is the reasonable cost. The device is typically listed between $250-$350, which is more affordable than most phone purchases. Another benefit to the iPad is the longevity of the device. Apple has a history of maintaining operating system support for its devices for at least four or five years, making your purchase worth the investment.

4. **Should I purchase an Android or iOS device?**

The short answer to this question is that it depends. If your district manages Android devices and provides Android training and resources, it might be a good idea to keep the same system in place rather than bring in a whole new operating system. Including all parties in the conversation increases the likelihood that the purchase will have more success and a quicker implementation process.

Successful Implementation

Bringing in the best resources available won't guarantee the correct use of the tools. We all have the technology graveyard, where old and sometimes new technology gets shoved into a closet due to tools becoming irrelevant or lack of expertise in using them. Preparing for the most success when implementing immersive technology will take research, planning, communication, training, and resources. The next chapter shares support for implementation that will help guide you and your team to success.

Learning Transported Challenge

Research and create a slideshow presenting the cost of your ideal immersive technology tools for your classroom. For a more advanced challenge, create a video tutorial on how to use an augmented, virtual, or mixed reality tool using some of the terms in this chapter.

Test out some of the tools listed in Appendix A and consider how you might share these experiences with your students given the infrastructure and device availability in your school. What are ways you can integrate the tools now? What are any roadblocks preventing you from using these tools in your classroom?

4 Successful Implementation

When beginning to implement immersive technology, the excitement often leads teachers to bring the tools into the classroom immediately, a natural "techie" move. Although you'll gain student engagement, you may not be able to get the full benefit without proper preparation. In past conversations with district administrators, the discussion rarely starts with an established plan of action. Many times, lack of knowledge about the difference between the immersive technologies is a barrier, but ultimately, the real difficulty is from the lack of direction. The conversation often ends without resolution because more thought is needed about the goals of the district, teachers, and students when using immersive technology. The discussion is resumed when a more precise plan of action is established.

Naturally, the following discussion pertains to a serious implementation. As we've discussed earlier, the initial barriers to using immersive technology are surprisingly low. It is expected that before a widespread and expensive adoption process even begins, teachers will have experimented with introductory and lower-bandwidth uses. It is also recommended that before serious departmental discussions begin, all personnel be given the opportunity to explore the basics of the technology.

Identify the Purpose

The first area to address when establishing a plan is identifying your purpose for bringing in immersive technology. Surprisingly, this question is the most difficult for educators to answer. The answer requires an explanation of the connection between immersive technology and educational benefit. Although there are an enormous amount of connections and benefits for our students in using these tools, effective educational use of the technologies requires research, experience and training.

One of the best ways to get buy-in for immersive technology is by bringing all parties in to the collaboration. The ideal situation is to get all the affected departments—classroom educators, technical support staff, and administrators—involved in order to gain greater support for the implementation and sustained use of the technology.

Classroom educators are the natural choice to connect the benefits to the needs of their students. Often, they are acutely aware of the current gaps in lessons and what types of resources would best address those gaps. The teacher identifies the limitations of his classroom while bridging the learning with current tools. In addition, the teacher knows the needs of her classroom and how the students prefer to learn (and how she prefers to teach). Without a classroom teacher being on board to implement immersive technology, the success is unlikely.

Support, conversation, and full buy-in with the **technology department** is the difference between easy implementation and frustration. The discussion with the technology department is important to decide which devices should be used for immersive technology experiences. The tech team will most certainly have an opinion on what technology can be easily adapted into the district infrastructure. An important topic with the tech department is network expectations for smooth implementation. There may be circumstances that prevent the use of all the tools. Without collaboration with the technology team, the educator would be left troubleshooting on their own.

Communication with the **instructional department** is a vital part in the sustainability of the technology. Although teachers may have the passion to implement the tools into the classroom, the link to the lesson plans and standards must be established. The instructional department provides the resources for the lessons, and the immersive technology tools may not fit with the plan. Substituting resources should be a district discussion that highlights the need for communication with all related parties.

Address Any Concerns

After establishing the reasons for using the technology in the classroom, the next step is addressing questions and issues that could arise from implementing the tools. If all departments are involved in the implementation from the initial stages, the potential problems were probably already presented in the discussion.

To help make the case for immersive technology adoption, **classroom educators** should be able to discuss which tools will directly address student needs. These tools can be justified with standards, student learning preferences, and student engagement. When the educator selects specific tools, the justification will be included in lesson plans.

The concerns of technology limitations or consistency should be handled by the **technology department**. They should be able to define the expectations of how often a teacher can run into issues and how quickly the technology team can fix potential barriers. Teachers should provide a list of specific tools they expect to use so that the technology department can prepare and test the tools in advance to minimize potential problems. It is important to note that although you may be able to run an immersive application in your classroom on your personal device with no issues, that same application may totally overwhelm the wireless network when you add a few student devices, or if the classroom next door accesses the network at the same time.

The concern over the effectiveness of the tools can be addressed by the **instructional team**, generally the administration. The department can determine how the implementation of the tools will be judged through assessment data, observations, and student feedback. They should also set goals and expectations for the technology use. Improving instruction through training and support for the tools should be consistently facilitated by the instructional team.

Be Flexible with Roles and Stress Teamwork

Although unforeseen circumstances may arise, the goal of teamwork and collaboration will benefit the expected outcomes for implementing immersive technology. When an individual is given the task to implement the tools for the whole district, the chances of problems and frustration increase. It is important to recognize that implementing a successful immersive technology program is a complex project that affects the entire system.

There are situations that arise in implementation where former instructional jobs are replaced with tasks such as cleaning and delivering devices, maintaining a calendar, and providing training for a single tool. When a district spends money on technology, it can affect positions as jobs are modified to make certain the technology is used. The problem with modifying a role for a specific tool is limiting the potential, influences and effectiveness of that individual. These problems can be alleviated by a teamwork approach and by giving roles to all involved to make the new technology manageable.

Consider the Space

When determining how to establish your classroom space, there are a few factors to consider when preparing for immersive lessons. The space should support the student with set boundaries, provide the best learning experiences, and give quick access to tools for frequent usage. Every classroom has a different setup, so each educator can adapt these recommendations to fit their needs. The most important things to take into consideration when planning classroom space for immersive technology are:

- Ability to charge devices

- Room for students to move and operate within the experience

- Sufficient lighting for camera and augmented reality function

One of the most essential areas to establish in your classroom is a charging station. The need for a charging station applies to classroom devices such as tablets, mobile devices, Chromebooks, and laptops. If you have access to multiple higher end devices such as HTC Vive, HoloLens, or even an Oculus Rift, you will need to have a place to charge these devices as well. It's ideal to keep the charging station in a secure location with easy access for classroom use, such as close proximity to the teacher desk.

Some technology allows the user to walk around a space while other technology locates the experience in a single space. Should your devices require space for movement, you will want to establish an open area to prevent collisions with other students or with classroom furniture. These problems generally occur when using virtual reality as there is no view of the physical space and objects around the person wearing the headset.

The space should allow the student to turn around and reach out with both arms, and it should provide some buffer space for movement throughout the experience as well. If the experience includes controllers, you will want to be aware that these items can potentially fly out the hands of the students. The HTC Vive requires approximately 130 square feet to get the full experience, which can take up a considerable amount of space. In addition, the Vive has four cameras and a cord from the viewer to the computer. Each experience requires a different amount of space, so plan to prepare your classroom accordingly.

Another consideration when planning your classroom setup is the lighting. While virtual reality won't be affected by the lighting in your room, the experiences in augmented and mixed reality depend heavily on the camera's device and view. An example of lighting issues is scanning augmented reality books. The lighting can especially affect a view if it creates a glare on objects that are scanned. Intense lighting can obstruct the camera's view of the target that must be detected to trigger the experience. Select an area that's not directly under a light or getting direct sunlight. Likewise, avoid areas that are dim and dark, which may hinder device cameras from detecting an image.

Training, Professional Development, & Personnel

The implementation of immersive technology requires training on the best ways to use the devices, the current tools available, and the most effective ways to prepare your class for a successful lesson. While the training can range from basic resources to hands-on creation tools, the implementation is dependent on educators feeling confident using the tools.

An effective training identifies the specific needs of the classroom and provides a resource to support those difficulties using AR, VR, or MR tools. The "wow" factor is exciting to get the interest of the students, but the depth of the learning will lead to continued use of the tools in a variety of ways. Sharing tools that can adapt to the variety of needs in the classroom provides the most beneficial training for the teacher.

Figure 4.1
Google Translate AR function.

Try It! Google Translate App

An example of a tool that can be used in multiple situations for classrooms is the augmented reality feature in Google Translate. The app can easily translate text into dozens of other languages while viewing it through your camera. To see this in action, open the Google Translate app, available from iTunes at **tiny.cc/translateapple** and Google Play at **tiny.cc/translateandroid**. Select the languages Spanish to English, then open the camera and point it at the image in Figure 4.1.

This tool presents an incredible opportunity for our students, teachers, and parents to have access to easy translation of written text. Imagine how students might benefit from this technology on their research projects and homework about other countries, or satisfy their curiosity and gain a deeper experience from exploring other cultures through documentaries or photo galleries. To add icing on the cake, you can download the languages inside the app so you don't need internet to use the translate feature. The versatility of this app makes it an essential tool for travelers as well.

Start Small, Be Accommodating, and Don't Forget to Play!

An early adopter of immersive technology may want to use tools that require little training to test their effectiveness. Bringing a variety of tools can feel overwhelming and require too much knowledge for one sitting. Start the trainings with a few tools that can benefit the classroom without overwhelming the audience. When educators begin to feel more comfortable with the tools, bring in a few more that can be easily adapted to different contexts.

Provide multiple resources in a variety of formats to accommodate the preferences of the educators. Having a face-to-face training may not be enough for some teachers who need to go back and reflect. Many educators prefer to have written directions to reference as they learn the tools. A short video can support some of the training with a quick tutorial while a written document can provide more specific directions and serve as a reference for later use.

Every campus has those tech rock stars that are willing to pick up a tool and try it out with their students immediately. The same teachers who are willing to deal with the glitches and bugs are often the teachers who can support their peers. The enthusiasm of the tech rock stars may give the nudge to other teachers to try the technology; their talents can also be useful at trainings and for support.

A solid training consists of relevant resources, includes a time to "play" with the tools, and provides a community to receive support with future implementation. The buy-in to immersive technology begins when educators see the relevance to their content area. The play time allows for questions, discussion, and problem solving on how to use the tool. The access to a community on the topic is an important resource for ideas, group support, and collaboration.

Adapting the Experience

Even after purchases are made, you may find that items such as viewers aren't used as often as you thought. Many times, the flow of the lesson limits students from using a viewer because it requires them to take the device out of the viewer to interact with an activity and then put it back in for the experience. While taking a device in and out of a viewer may be acceptable on occasion, it dampens the full experience. In these cases, teachers should stop using the viewer unless it allows for more immersion without distractions.

Although experiences can be enhanced with specific technology available, there will be tools for some interactive activities to supplement depending on your resources. If a classroom is limited to desktop computers, laptops, or Chromebooks but would like to engage in immersive activities, there are some alternatives to support the lesson that may not be as intense.

The resources most beneficial with computers and laptops are virtual reality activities that can be experienced in the browser. These activities give 360° views to explore learning and are beginning to be found in some web based education companies' websites. Although the alternative resource may not capture the attention of the students in the same way as using a viewer, the personalized learning is still key as the student takes control of their view.

An example of an alternative resource is in the Chapter 5 lesson plan on the solar system. The lesson uses augmented reality on a mobile device to walk through the solar system. The students will see the differences and similarities of the planets and the sun while collecting the radius of each object. The lesson is intended to walk through the solar system using a mobile device, however, as an alternative, students can view the solar system in 3D within their browser at **solarsystemscope. com**. An increased flexibility in alternative activities is growing to correspond with the rising demand for cross-platform devices.

Selecting the Right Classroom Tools

Although the fancy single-user systems are the current darlings of the media, the much more affordable and useful (for the classroom) VR systems are very exciting and productive in their own right. There are a number of advantages, beginning with affordability, that directly lead to more access for students. Rather than having the entire class wait as a single student has an experience, everyone can participate at once. Another big advantage of the lower-cost solutions is that because of the much higher adoption rates, there is already a huge library of educational content that can be accessed freely or at little cost.

Although you can explore limited versions of immersive technologies with nothing more than your existing classroom computers or tablets, taking the next step in VR is also relatively inexpensive and easy. Some schools may already have devices such as smartphones or iPads available, either as district-provided or student-owned sets. Even if your school doesn't yet take advantage of these ubiquitous resources, the cost of providing them is modest, especially if you allow students to use their own equipment.

Once you have the portable devices you need, the next piece is choosing a viewer. The good news here is that the basic technology used in the headsets is minimal and thus they've already become a commodity item, often included with new cellphones or available for about the cost of stereo headphones.

Select the Best Viewer

Prior to making a purchase for a viewer, there are several factors to consider that don't seem obvious at first glance. Although the term "viewer" can vary based on the technology, my definition of a viewer for the purposes of this book is the case that holds a mobile device. Often, the viewer is described as goggles, a headset, a head-mounted display (HMD), or cardboard.

A commonality between VR viewers are the biconvex lenses. The converging lens is symmetrical in form. The distance between our mobile devices and the viewer is much too close for our eyes to view the experience without losing focus and putting a strain on your eyes. In other words, the lens helps us focus on the screen when it is sitting so close to our eyes. A viewer without the proper lens is a terrible experience.

Most viewers look similar, but their features often vary. Some of the most important and least important features are covered below to support districts in making informed purchases. Although the viewer is not a critical purchase, the decisions on which features you choose will affect which of the apps you can use.

Material

One of the most affordable VR viewers is Google's Cardboard, and yes, it is made of cardboard. The surge of popularity for virtual reality on our mobile devices can largely be attributed to the affordability of a VR viewer. Google's introductory advertisement urging us to experience virtual reality in a cardboard viewer may have

	Sanitizable	Selection Button	Adjustable Lenses	Exposed Camera	Shock Absorbent	Comfortable	Cost
MERGE VR	👓	👓	👓	👓	👓	👓	$60
DAYDREAM		👓				👓	$79
VIEW-MASTER	👓	👓				👓	$29
COBRA VR	👓			👓			$15
CARDBOARD		👓		👓			$2

What are you looking for in a viewer?

Figure 4.2

Comparing the preferred features in a viewer.

seemed far-reaching to some, but the concept took off quickly because it was easily adaptable and dirt cheap.

The concept of cardboard may be the brilliance that started this revolution, but it's certainly not the best option for our classrooms. Most educators recognize that a cardboard viewer won't last long with students. What's even more important to consider than the short lifespan of cardboard is the issue of safety.

A cardboard viewer attracts germs because it contacts the user's eyes, nose, and ears. The material absorbs sweat, tears, condensed moisture, and oils from your face. Dead skin cells collect on the cardboard and you have the added chance of exposure to germs. The cardboard material doesn't allow the viewer to be sanitized without warping the material. The cardboard viewer is a fantastic individual solution, but not a practical option for a classroom.

I was told a story where a family member received a new Google Pixel phone and a Daydream viewer for Christmas. The family enjoyed sharing the experience together and each person in the family took part in the fun. While the thought to disinfect the viewer never crossed their minds, the dangers were present even within the family. Within a few days, all the family members were infected with pink eye.

Transferring pink eye or other infections from one student to another can happen quickly. To avoid situations such as this, the planning and preparation to disinfect viewers should be a top priority. When preparing a budget for immersive technology purchases, consumable cleaning products should be included. Fortunately, almost every basic viewer is quite affordable, which should allow most schools to provide each student with their own viewer. Even if each student has their personal viewer, they still should be disinfected and cleaned regularly.

Magnetic Selection Button

While using immersive technology apps, the need to select and manipulate items on the screen is often part of the experience. However, because the device is housed inside the viewer, users can't directly touch the screen or device buttons. Many viewers have a magnetic selection button located on the outside of the unit. The selection button on a viewer is similar to clicking with a mouse on a computer. Instead of scrolling around the screen with a mouse, the individual views the screen in 360° by moving up, down, left, and right. The location of the selection button can be on the side or top of the viewer. The button is typically a magnet that slides, letting the device know that a choice has been made. In order to select items on the screen, most apps require the user to touch the device screen or slide the magnet to "click" on the screen.

This feature works best when the viewer is matched with a specific model of device, for instance, when using a Samsung phone with a Samsung headset or one from another company made specifically for that phone. Generic viewers with this feature can be hit-or-miss with some devices so you'll want to test various combinations. Although there are some alternatives, you don't want to eliminate apps from your classroom due to a missing selection tool.

Button control isn't mandatory, however, highly interactive experiences will require a selection tool or controller to engage with the content in the app. Some apps allow the user to stare at a specific area for an extended period of time to make the selection. Check to see what the experience requires before choosing a viewer.

Using an external controller eliminates the need for a selection button, however, not all devices work with controllers. Apple devices have not been as compatible with controllers used with AR, VR, and MR apps. Some mixed reality apps will use a handheld controller.

Adjustable View

Another factor in determining the right viewer is the strap to hold the viewer in place. There are times that the interaction within the app requires students to hold on to a controller or use the selection button. In this case, a head strap to hold the device in place while using your hands for interaction may be necessary. The strap presents another issue of sanitation as it straps around the student's head and hair. We don't pass a hat around for our students to share, nor would we pass around a viewer before sanitizing the straps.

The benefit of a head strap is the free use of both hands while in the app. Having both hands available is specifically important for augmented and mixed reality experiences where a controller is used or a cube is being held and rotated in the camera view. A head strap is not always required and should be avoided in some interactive experiences, especially when the device is often swapped in and out of the viewer.

Make sure your viewer has an adjustable head strap, as head sizes vary. Asking a student to wear the viewer when the straps are too large could create slipping of the viewer during the experience and could potentially cause the device to fall. A strap that is too small could create a strain on the student's face and possibly eliminate some students from participating. An adjustable strap provides the flexibility for all students to enjoy the experience while also protecting the device.

The flexibility of being able to adjust the lens location to accommodate students' varied vision is a must. When an experience is hindered by a fuzzy, out-of-focus view, frustration builds and you've lost the "wow" of immersive technology. Many times, students are so engaged by the experience that they continue even though it can be a bit fuzzy. Even during a fairly short session, out-of-focus viewers can give students a headache by putting strain on their eyes. The immersive experience is dependent on a clear view, and the adjustment of the lens on a viewer is vital to provide access for all students. Although some students who wear prescription eyeglasses can use the focus features in a viewer to get a clear image without their glasses, some will need to keep their glasses on. Not all viewers are comfortable to wear when also wearing eyeglasses, and some won't accommodate them at all.

Another consideration when deciding on the right viewer is the size of devices that the viewer holds. In some cases, a viewer is designated for a specific model of phone. Selecting a viewer for the appropriate device is similar to selecting the right protective case for a phone. Most viewers have a general size that accommodates the most popular devices, but doing the research to confirm the viewer is compatible with the device is essential.

Exposed Camera

In a virtual reality experience, the use of the camera is unnecessary because VR doesn't layer objects on our real world but immerses the individual into a completely digital view instead. Augmented and mixed reality apps, however, do require the use of the camera, and selecting the right viewer should include a cut out for the camera to be exposed.

Many viewers cover the camera as they are only intended for virtual reality apps. Although virtual reality may be the immediate use of the tools, you don't want to be limited by your viewer. Selecting a camera-friendly viewer will open the possibilities for different types of experiences.

Optional Features

Two key optional features I recommend considering are comfort and shock absorbency. These are considered optional only in that they don't directly affect performance or limit (or expand) the types of apps you can run.

Comfort is an issue, especially if you intend to run longer simulations or will often run multiple apps in succession. Obviously, comfort is somewhat subjective and in many instances can be affected by the level and ease of adjustment of the straps. Some viewers are designed with pads intended to shift some of the weight onto the forehead, which can make wearing the device much more bearable during longer sessions.

Because the viewers themselves are relatively inexpensive, have few moving parts, and are relatively robust, it isn't the viewer that shock absorbency is intended to protect. The device that is placed inside can be hundreds of times more costly than the viewer, and is almost always much more fragile. When installed within a shock absorbent viewer, an expensive cell phone or other device is somewhat protected from falls.

Network Limitations

Although the choices of headsets, devices, and applications are the first things that many educators considering immersive technologies think of, the reality is that your network infrastructure needs to be considered first.

When frequent internet disruptions occur, the immersive activity can quickly change from engaged to frustrated. If a student has diligently scanned a 3D object only to have nothing happen because the network is down, it could destroy even the best of lessons. Some apps require a consistent internet connection to function properly, and these tools should only be used with a dependable network.

Be aware that there are many factors that can affect your network reliability, particularly wireless network access. Your school may have adequate bandwidth, but perhaps the access point for your classroom is too far away or obstructed by walls. Other factors that could affect signal strength are district usage, weather, and interference from other wireless transmissions. Verify the signal strength on your classroom devices and if the signal is too low, try improving your location and eliminating interference. Also check to see if neighboring classrooms are heavily accessing the network.

Depending on the app, the demand on the network can be considerable. When the usage is at a peak, all users will experience a slowdown. Finding the right tools when the demand is high will support a better experience without frequent pauses or crashing. In most cases, limiting how many devices are running at the same time in the classroom can help reduce problems. Determine how many devices are necessary for the lesson at a single time to avoid slowing down the network.

Fortunately, many applications require little to no internet connection. Others allow you to download the experience in advance rather than streaming content, meaning you can download to a few devices at a time and, once all the devices have the experience downloaded, they can run it without an internet connection.

Of course, many classrooms have wired internet connections, at least to a few classroom computers. These connections are typically much more robust than wireless connections. The key is to test your network environment. Remember, you may find that what worked flawlessly on your own device when you tested it after school won't even come close to working on 20 or more devices simultaneously in the middle of the school day!

When you find the limitations of your network, share your findings with your principal or the technical support staff in your school. They may have solutions or may be willing to invest in additional network resources.

Individual Tools

Although the emphasis throughout this book is on mobile devices and tools that can be easily accessed or acquired for the classroom, some may find themselves in the situation of considering a higher end device purchase. There are many factors to take into account when choosing an individual tool such as the HTC Vive or Microsoft HoloLens, both of which are briefly discussed here.

HTC Vive

The success of the HTC Vive has brought wide-scale attention to virtual reality. The Vive headset is attached by a cord to a powerful computer with an unusually high-powered graphics card. The experience in a Vive is completely immersive as the 360° view is crystal clear and the directional sound gives you the feeling that you're really there. The setup requires enough space in a room for the user to walk around and has a camera located in each corner to identify the space. Although the experience on the Vive is remarkable, the cost (about $700 for the headset and controllers) and the required space, combined with the "one user at a time" limit don't make this tool ideal in a classroom.

Microsoft HoloLens

Another notable device that uses mixed reality is the Microsoft HoloLens. The current cost is $3,000 but, unlike the Vive, the HoloLens is fully self-contained with a computer that Microsoft claims is more powerful than many laptops on the market. Another difference is that the HoloLens is truly mobile; it doesn't require a dedicated space and doesn't need to be connected to a computer. Its biggest advantage in the classroom is the promised partnerships between Microsoft and various media and publishing companies. In fact, companies like Lifeliqe have already created augmented, virtual, and mixed reality experiences for the device in connection with classroom curriculum. As these devices come down in price, it's a good bet that we'll see this technology grow in classrooms.

Here are some questions an educator must resolve when determining if an individual tool is appropriate for their classroom:

- When a student is experiencing the device, what would the other students be doing?
- Where will the space be located?
- Is there sufficient bandwidth and/or a powerful enough computer available to run the equipment?

- Who is qualified to run the computer when the student is using the device?

- What content is available to run on the device?

Although these tools may not be suitable for a classroom today, the technology is leading the way toward future devices that are more flexible and cost effective. For educators, it is important to realize that this level of highly productive immersive technology tools exists and that, even though the top-end devices might not yet be practical, we can still prepare our students by introducing them to the concepts and devices we can afford today.

Putting It All Together

The best option to begin using augmented, virtual, and mixed reality is to use the tools that are already in the classroom. Instead of waiting for funding and resources to play and learn with immersive technology, begin using the tools you have available now. With an enormous library of resources that can be used on a variety of platforms, there's no reason to hold off using immersive technology while waiting for a future purchase.

Learning Transported Challenge

Create a poster with classroom expectations that apply to immersive technology tools for the most successful immersive technology experiences.

Design a presentation that describes your immersive technology implementation plan for your school or district. Address the purpose, the selected devices, the viewers, and how you plan to have the most successful immersive technology experiences.

5 Getting Started Experiencing AR and VR

Many immersive technology apps are available and selecting the tools that fit a specific grade, content area, and learning objective will make the resources more relevant. The following lesson plans share distinctive ways that immersive technology can support the learning in the classroom. Although the lesson plans in this chapter are listed with specific standards and objectives, they can be modified to fit various needs in the classroom. All of the lessons feature apps that are compatible with mobile devices and/or computers. For more information about the tools used in the lessons, refer to Appendix A in the back of this book.

Elementary Ideas K–5

The elementary lessons include apps that will get your students involved with exploring and creating. Beginning with the app CoSpaces, the students design 3D objects to demonstrate mathematical knowledge of geometry. The next lesson includes an activity that uses augmented reality to provide a realistic scene for storytelling in Storyfab. The final lesson uses the EON Creator app to explore the Earth's properties.

Virtual Shapes

DEVICE: iOS / Android / Chromebook / PC

COURSE: Math, Geometry

GRADE: 2–5

STANDARDS ADDRESSED

Standards for Mathematical Practice

2.G.A.1: Recognize and draw shapes having specified attributes, such as a given number of angles or a given number of equal faces. Identify triangles, quadrilaterals, pentagons, hexagons, and cubes.

3.G.A.1: Understand that shapes in different categories (e.g., rhombuses, rectangles, and others) may share attributes (e.g., having four sides), and that the shared attributes can define a larger category (e.g., quadrilaterals). Recognize rhombuses, rectangles, and squares as examples of quadrilaterals, and draw examples of quadrilaterals that do not belong to any of these subcategories.

4.G.A.2: Classify two-dimensional figures based on the presence or absence of parallel or perpendicular lines, or the presence or absence of angles of a specified size. Recognize right triangles as a category, and identify right triangles.

5.G.B.4: Classify two-dimensional figures in a hierarchy based on properties.

TIME: 60 MINUTE LESSON

DESCRIPTION

The lesson begins with the students planning out their space on paper. The space will include three-sided to eight-sided objects. After the space has been planned, students will use the app CoSpaces to organize and categorize various shapes. The virtual reality space allows students to easily drag and drop objects to a plane that can be shared with a simple link for others to view. Students will categorize 2D objects and 3D objects based on faces and vertices.

OBJECTIVE

- The students will be able to identify and categorize various shapes.

- The students will be able to describe and name shapes in the environment.

- The students will be able to differentiate between 2- and 3-dimensional objects.

- The students will be able to determine the number of angles and sides for 2-dimensional objects and faces, vertices, and edges for 3-dimensional objects.

Virtual Shapes

MATERIALS

Computer or mobile device (iOS or Android)

Virtual reality viewer (optional)

Disinfectant wipes or cleaner (when using viewers)

Writing tools

CoSpaces accounts (teacher and classroom account). Get the app from iTunes at **tiny.cc/cospacesandroid** and Google Play at **tiny.cc/cospacesandroid**.

Procedure

The teacher will begin by sharing an example of a virtual world created in CoSpaces that include s 2D and 3D objects.
(5 minutes)

The teacher will briefly explain how to use CoSpaces and the expectations for the students. (5 minutes)

The students will draw out a rough draft of their space using 2D and 3D objects. (10 minutes)

The students will login to their free account Maker (or paid classroom account EDU) at CoSpaces.io and select "Create Space." (5 minutes)

The students will design their space and drag and drop objects into the plane. By selecting Library and Web Image Search, the students can search for specific 2D and 3D objects. (20 minutes)

The students can share their space with the class and the teacher by link or by QR code on the computer. It's important for the students to name the space by going back to the main page and typing their name. The teacher can also view these spaces inside of the classroom account. (5 minutes)

The students can view these spaces in a mobile device by typing in the URL into the browser and allowing it to be opened in the app. (10 minutes)

Assessment

The students will be evaluated based the rough draft and final space in CoSpaces.

RUBRIC				
CATEGORY	4	3	2	1
Rough Draft	Rough draft was completed with 2D and 3D shapes listed and categorized.	Rough draft was completed with 2D and 3D shapes listed and but not categorized.	Rough draft was incomplete but included some 2D and 3D shapes listed and categorized.	Rough draft was incomplete and didn't include any 2D or 3D shapes listed.
Requirements	All requirements are met and exceeded in CoSpaces.	All requirements are met in CoSpaces.	One require-ment was not completely met in CoSpaces.	More than one requirement was not com-pletely met in CoSpaces.
Organization	Content is well organized using headings or texts to list object categories.	Use headings or texts to list and organize, but the overall organi-zation of objects appears flawed.	Content is logi-cally organized for the most part.	There was no clear or logical organizational structure, just lots of objects.
Content	Covers topic in-depth with details and examples. Subject knowledge is excellent.	Includes essential knowledge about the topic. Subject knowledge appears to be good.	Includes essential information about the topic but there are 1 or 2 factual errors.	Content is min-imal or there are several factual errors.

Modifications

Provide templates for students when drawing out their rough draft of their space.

Provide visual representation of 2D and 3D shapes to reference as needed in the project.

Provide a predesigned space in CoSpaces that students can modify and categorize the 2D and 3D shapes.

Enrichment

Ask students to list the number of faces, vertices or edges in 3D objects and parallel sides, equal side or angles in 2D shapes.

Figure 5.1
CoSpaces egg

The students can add 3D shapes that are made of many 2D shapes. An example is a student showing that a 3D egg is made of multiple 2D triangles.

Storytelling

DEVICE: iOS / Android

COURSE: English Language Arts, Speaking and Listening

GRADE: K-1

STANDARDS ADDRESSED

English Language Arts Standards

SL.K.4: Describe familiar people, places, things, and events and, with prompting and support, provide additional detail.

SL.K.5: Add drawings or other visual displays to descriptions as desired to provide additional detail.

SL.1.4: Describe people, places, things, and events with relevant details, expressing ideas and feelings clearly.

SL.1.5: Add drawings or other visual displays to descriptions when appropriate to clarify ideas, thoughts, and feelings.

TIME: 55 MINUTE LESSON

DESCRIPTION

The students create videos in the Storyfab app. The students begin by drawing a picture of a beach as their trigger image. After the teacher gives directions on how to use the app, the students will open one of the prebuilt scenes with the pirates. The students can use animation in the story that fits in the story with each character mood. The students can also change the props in the scene to support the story plot. The students will record a story that can be planned or impromptu using the three characters in the scene.

The students will describe "who" is in the story, "what" is happening in the story, and "where" the story is located within the recording.

OBJECTIVES

- The student will be able to create a drawing and customize the scene related to the story.

- The student will be able to describe the people, place, things and events in the story.

- The students will be able to describe feelings and context using animation and digital objects.

MATERIALS

Mobile device (iOS)

Storyfab app, found at tiny.cc/storyfab

Writing and drawing tools (high contrast colors work best)

Storyfab account, if desired (teacher account logged in to devices using Facebook)

Procedure

The teacher will begin by sharing an example of a story in Storyfab. (5 minutes)

The teacher will briefly explain how to use Storyfab and ask students to watch the brief "Getting Started" Intro and Setup videos. (5 minutes)

The students will draw a beach scene that has contrasting colors. It can help to add black outlines to drawings. (15 minutes)

The students will open the app and select the clapperboard at the bottom of the screen and select "skip" if no account is signed in. The students will select the pirate scene. The students will hold the device parallel to the drawing on their paper until the scene loads. The students will select the green check mark when the scene loads correctly. (5 minutes)

The students will remain looking at the paper while adjusting items in the scene. The characters and props can get selected and moved into new spaces. The characters can change their animation, expression by selecting the character and then selecting any of the items at the bottom of the screen. (5 minutes)

The students will begin recording after they have established the animation for the scene by selecting the red circle on the screen. After the countdown, students will begin speaking for the characters while the animation is running. Students can record several scenes from multiple angles with a variety of animations. When the story is complete, the students will select the box with arrows at the bottom to save the story. (20 minutes)

Many teachers have had a chance to put Storyfab into their lessons to give our students the opportunity to share their knowledge using 3D objects to record a video. Assistant Principal, Kristen Dutschmann of China Springs ISD in Texas shared how students can create book trailers to advertise their favorite books in the library with their classmates. She added that stories are a great way for students to practice summarizing skills, especially when describing historical events.

Storytelling

The students can save the story by selecting the sharing symbol under the video and save the video to the camera roll. (5 minutes)

Assessment

The students will be evaluated based on the following criteria.

RUBRIC				
CATEGORY	4	3	2	1
Drawing	The student turns in an attractive drawing of the beach using contrasting colors.	The student turns in a completed drawing of the beach using contrasting colors.	The student turns in an incomplete drawing with or without a beach.	The student did not complete a drawing.
Vocabulary	Uses a varied vocabulary appropriate to answer the who, what and where of the story.	Uses some vocabulary appropriate to answer the who, what and where of the story.	Uses little vocabulary appropriate to answer the who, what and where of the story.	Uses no vocabulary appropriate to answer the who, what and where of the story.
Characters	The characters are clearly described (through words and actions).	The characters are described (through words or actions).	The characters are somewhat described. The audience knows very little about the characters.	It is hard to tell the character roles.
Setting	The scene adds meaning to the story.	The scene supports the story.	The scene somewhat supports the story.	The scene doesn't support the story.

Modifications

Provide an image for students to use as their trigger image.

Provide visuals of the characters before beginning.

Provide visuals to show the steps to create the video.

Provide a storyboard sheet to help students prepare to answer Who, What, and Where in their story.

Enrichment

Have students create characters that reflect themselves.

Ask students to modify the characters and props in the pirate scene to change the plot.

The students can build the characters and props from scratch using the blank scene.

Augmented and Virtual Reality with EON

- **DEVICE:** iOS / Android
- **COURSE:** Earth and Space Science
- **GRADE:** 4

STANDARDS ADDRESSED

Next Generation Science Standards

4-ESS2-2: Analyze and interpret data from maps to describe patterns of Earth's features.

TIME: 45 MINUTE LESSON

DESCRIPTION

The students will explore the Earth's properties using 3D objects, augmented, and virtual reality. The lesson shows views of Earth's components, including continents and oceans.

OBJECTIVE

- The student will be able to describe the four main structures in the Earth's structure.

- The student will be able to locate the different land and water features areas of Earth.

MATERIALS

Mobile device or tablet with the EON Creator App from iOS at **tiny.cc/eoncreatorapple** or Google Play at **tiny.cc/eoncreatorandroid**

EON Creator account

Trigger Image from Figure 5.2 or **tinyurl.com/ybwm4rnx**

 WORLD'S LEADING VR KNOWLEDGE TRANSFER SOFTWARE

 WORLD'S LARGEST VR LEARNING LIBRARY

 36 MILLION USERS

 WORLD'S LARGEST VR DEVELOPMENT NETWORK

www.eonreality.com/**vrex**

Figure 5.2

EON Creator trigger image.

Procedure

The class will begin with writing a prediction about the Earth's layers in a notebook. (10 minutes)

The teacher briefly discusses and provides the vocabulary of the Earth's features. (5 minutes)

The students will go through the Earth Science Lesson and Earth System Course in EON Creator to view the Earth in 3D and interact with its various features. (20 minutes)

The lesson will conclude with a write-up of the accuracy of the prediction. (10 minutes)

Modifications

Provide sentence starters for the predictions.

Provide a visual of the Earth's layers and features.

Enrichment

Ask students to recreate a 3D model of the earth using play-doh.

Ask students to draw the Earth's layers in the concluding write-up.

The students in Dr. Harvey's classroom from Nanjing China were able to use the EON Creator App to explore details from organs. One student said "wow, I can see what the teacher meant!" During the lesson, the students were able to explore the learning in a more authentic way with the content from the pages coming alive. The EON Creator app allows students to participate in the lesson beyond what they would normally do in a 2D setting. Dr. Harvey explains that due to the nature of the content, he was able to ask students to describe the functionality of the organs and the physical processes taken place in the body.

"Immersive technology allows, at least in science, to see abstract concepts in a more concrete form." (Harvey, 2017). The interactions were much more engaging because the boring content on a page had deeper meaning when provided in 3D. The EON lesson gave Dr. Harvey's students an appreciation of the complexity of the body system.

Secondary Ideas 6–12

The secondary lessons include interactions that support learning with the use of augmented and virtual reality. The first lesson uses a virtual reality app to practice public speaking. The next lesson will let the students walk around the solar system to explore the relative sizes of the planets in comparison to the whole solar system. The final lesson uses the EON Creator app to explore the circulatory, respiratory and the digestive system using augmented and virtual reality.

Public Speaking with Virtual Speech

DEVICE: iOS / Android

COURSE: English / Language Arts, Listening and Speaking

GRADE: Middle School

STANDARDS ADDRESSED

English Language Arts Standards

SL.6.6: Adapt speech to a variety of contexts and tasks, demonstrating command of formal English when indicated or appropriate.

SL.7.6: The student will be able to adapt speech to a variety of context and tasks, demonstrating command of formal English when indicated or appropriate.

SL.8.6: Adapt speech to a variety of contexts and tasks, demonstrating command of formal English when indicated or appropriate.

TIME: 45 MINUTES LESSON. (Presentations vary based on class size.)

DESCRIPTION

The students will practice writing and presenting on a topic about their future careers. The presentation will be shared in a variety of contexts such as peer-to-peer, virtual, and whole classroom.

OBJECTIVE

- The student will compose and speak real experiences using descriptive details and a structured outline.

- The student will write a persuasive piece using convincing vocabulary.

MATERIALS

Mobile iOS or Android device

Virtual Speech app (downloaded onto device from iOS Store at **tiny.cc/virtual-speechapple** or Google Play at **tiny.cc/virtualspeechandroid**)

Virtual reality viewer with a selection tool (typically a button or magnet)

Disinfectant wipes or cleaner to use when sharing viewers

Writing tools

Procedure

The teacher will begin by sharing a short description about themselves to the class. They will share a skill that they use in their current profession. (5 minutes)

The students will write a short description about themselves listing a skill they have and plan to use in a future career. The length should be limited to two paragraphs. (15 minutes)

In partners, students will share their key points with one another twice. The length of each speech should be limited to 2 minutes. (10 minutes)

One student will practice their speech in the Virtual Speech app (using the classroom scene) while the partner will support with reminders of the key points if needed. (15 minutes)

The final part of the lesson will be the classroom presentation. (Time varies)

Assessment

The students will be evaluated based on their performance in groups and individual class presentations.

RUBRIC				
CATEGORY	4	3	2	1
Collaboration with Peers	Listens to, shares with, and supports the efforts of their partner.	Mostly listens to, shares with, and supports the efforts of their partner.	Somewhat listens to, shares with, and supports the efforts of their partner.	Didn't support their partner.
Listens to Other Presentations	Listens intently. Does not make distracting noises or movements.	Listens intently but has some distracting noises or movement.	Sometimes does not appear to be listening but is not distracting.	Sometimes does not appear to be listening and has distracting noises or movements.

Stays on Topic	Stays on topic all (100%) of the time.	Stays on topic most (99-90%) of the time.	Stays on topic some (89%-75%) of the time.	It was hard to tell what the topic was.
Speaks Clearly	Speaks clearly and distinctly all (100-95%) the time, and mispronounces no words.	Speaks clearly and distinctly all (100-95%) the time, but mispronounces one word.	Speaks clearly and distinctly most (94-85%) of the time. Mispronounces no more than one word.	Often mumbles or cannot be understood OR mispronounces more than one word.

Modifications

In preparation for sharing the description with the class, the students will have the option to watch the short video, "Overcome Your Fear of Speaking" in the Virtual Speech app to learn how to confidently connect with their audience.

Provide a computer to watch "Learn How to Overcome the Fear of Public Speaking" at **youtu.be/NVFtWOKQXyo**

Write an outline of key points.

Figure 5.3
Students using Virtual Speech app

Enrichment

Select more settings in Virtual Speech to adapt the presentation to a variety of audiences.

Add personalized slides in Virtual Speech by adding in your own presentation when following these instructions iOS and Android.

The students from Mrs. Rachelle Dene Poth's class in Pennsylvania enjoyed practicing Spanish using the Virtual Speech app. The students stated it was "cool" to present to an audience that felt real. They felt it was a great way to become more comfortable speaking and preparing for speeches in a unique way. Some of the students expressed their wish that they were aware of the product last year before getting in front of large crowds.

Walking in the Solar System with the Solar App

DEVICE: iOS / Android

COURSE: Science, Earth's Place in the Universe, Analyzing and Interpreting Data

GRADE: Middle School

STANDARDS ADDRESSED

MS-ESS1-3: Analyze and interpret data to determine scale properties of objects in the solar system.

English Language Arts Standards

RST.6-8.1 Cite specific textual evidence to support analysis of science and technical texts.

RST.6-8.7 Integrate quantitative or technical information expressed in words in a text with a version of that information expressed visually (e.g., in a flowchart, diagram, model, graph, or table).

Standards for Mathematical Practice

MP.2 Reason abstractly and quantitatively.

6.RP.A.1 Understand the concept of a ratio and use ratio language to describe a ratio relationship between two quantities.

7.RP.A.2 Recognize and represent proportional relationships between quantities.

TIME: 45 MINUTE LESSON

DESCRIPTION

The pairs of students will walk around the solar system using augmented reality through a mobile device. The students will take note the visual differences and similarities in the objects in the solar system. The students will collect the data on planets and the sun as described in the Solar app. The students will list the radius of the objects in ascending order in a table.

OBJECTIVE
- The student will use data analysis to compare the relationships of the size of the plants in relation to one another and the sun.

- The student will recognize and represent data to show the similarities and differences of the objects in the solar system.

MATERIALS

Mobile iOS or Android device. If not enough devices are available, create larger groups. Solar app downloaded onto device from iTunes Store or Google Play (or at **aireal.io/producthunt?ref=producthunt**)

If no mobile devices are available, experience a 3D representation of the solar system that includes more data on a computer at at **solarsystemscope.com**.

Writing tools

Procedure

The teacher will begin by sharing a short description about the Solar app and how to open the experience and select the location settings necessary to participate. The teacher will set up students in pairs. (10 minutes)

The pairs of students will walk around the solar system in the mobile app taking note of the radius of the sun and planets. If the students are on a computer they can collect the same data at **solarsystemscope.com**. One of the students will show the experience on a mobile device while the other student writes down the data. Halfway through the experience, the students will switch roles. (20 minutes)

In partners, students will collect and write their data in ascending order in a table of the radius of the plants and the sun. (15 minutes)

Assessment

The students will be evaluated based on their performance in groups and individual table calculations and data.

RUBRIC				
CATEGORY	4	3	2	1
Participation	Used time well in experience and focused attention on comparing and contrasting the relationship of objects.	Used time pretty well. Stayed focused on the experience most of the time.	Did the experience but did not appear very interested. Focus was lost on several occasions.	Participation was minimal OR student was uninterested in participating.
RUBRIC continued				

Walking in the Solar System with the Solar App

CATEGORY	4	3	2	1
Data Collection	Clear, accurate, dated data is taken.	Dated, clear, accurate data is taken, but didn't include all data.	Data is taken, but accuracy of information is questionable and didn't include all data.	Very little data was taken or of little use.
Results/ Calculations	The results/ calculations are correct and labeled appropriately.	Most results/ calculations are correct and labeled appropriately.	Some results/ calculations are correct and the results labeled appropriately.	No results/ calculations are shown OR results are inaccurate or mislabeled.
Data	Professional looking and accurate representation of the data in tables and/or graphs. Graphs and tables are labeled and titled.	Accurate representation of the data in tables and/or graphs. Graphs and tables are labeled and titled.	Accurate representation of the data in written form, but no graphs or tables are presented.	Data are not shown OR are inaccurate.

Modifications

Provide a pre-built table that includes some of the locations of the planets and their radius.

Print out the data on the radius of the planets in larger text to supplement the experience.

Provide written directions of each step and space to fill in the information.

Enrichment

Ask students to create a table in ascending order that lists the objects distance from the sun and write it in scientific notation.

Ask students to create a diagram of the solar system using proportions to describe the size of the planets in comparison to the sun.

Students in Denis Wright's classroom from Ocean Bay Middle School, South Carolina used the Solar app to engage with science content. The experience brought fun into the lesson, however, the request to have realistic proportions of the planets was requested by the students.

Augmented and Virtual Reality with EON

DEVICE: iOS / Android

COURSE: Life Science

GRADE: 9-10

STANDARDS ADDRESSED

Next Generation Science Standards

HS-LS1-2: Develop and use a model to illustrate the hierarchical organization of interacting systems that provide specific functions within multicellular organisms.

TIME: 60-120 MINUTE LESSON

DESCRIPTION

The students will explore the circulatory, respiratory and the digestive system within the EON Creator app. In the app, students will view the various body systems using augmented and virtual reality. While exploring the systems, students can view the organs in 3D, x-ray view and layered on top of the trigger image.

OBJECTIVE

- The student will be able to identify the internal structures of the human heart and understand their functions.

- The student will be able to identify the different parts of the respiratory system and explore their functions.

- The student will be able to explore the complete process in the digestive system and explain the role of different organs involved in the digestive process.

MATERIALS

Mobile device or tablet with the EON Creator App from iOS at **tiny.cc/eoncreatorapple** or Google Play at **tiny.cc/eoncreatorandroid**

EON Creator account

Trigger Image from EON (From Figure 5.2 on page 43, or at the following link.)

cdn4.eonreality.com/wp-content/uploads/2016/01/QRMARKER-NEW.png

Augmented and Virtual Reality with EON

Procedure

The teacher will begin by discussing and providing the vocabulary of the circulatory, respiratory, and digestive systems. (10 minutes)

The teacher will have students in groups (with each group given a device) collaborate and work together in the EON experience. (5 minutes)

The students will go through the Human Life Processes lesson. The quantity of time will depend on how much the students will engage in the activities. Students will change who is holding the device each time they move to a new body system. (40-60 minutes)

The lesson includes interactive activities and quizzes to confirm understanding. (20 minutes)

Modifications

The students are evaluated within the EON app. The assessment activities are Locate, Quiz, and Build.

Assessment

Provide a vocabulary list of the circulatory, respiratory and the digestive system to use with the app.

Provide a visual of the body systems and label the various parts.

Enrichment

Ask students to create a visual of the body systems as they relate to the whole body.

Ask students to give a presentation of the circulatory, respiratory, and digestive systems to the whole class. Display the app on a projector and allow the student to use the 3D objects to describe the systems.

Keep Going

With the influx of immersive technology tools becoming available, we are likely to see more that are tailored for classroom experiences. The lessons shared here are an entry point into what promises to be a growing field for educators looking to add these rich learning experiences to their daily lessons.

By serving as early adopters, you are helping add to the available pool of information around using virtual, augmented, and mixed reality in the classroom. I encourage you to share with others—in your school or PLN, or on Twitter using the #ARVRinEDU hashtag—your experience of sharing these or other lessons with your students. What modifications would you make? How would you adapt the lesson or tool for your content area?

Learning Transported Challenge

Design a lesson that includes an interactive augmented and virtual reality tool specifically designed for your content area. Browse the tools in the appendix or the activity ideas in Chapter 6 for inspiration.

For a more advanced challenge, create your own multi-user interactive lesson in the EON Creator app and invite your students to participate.

6 Open Collaboration and Exploration

Although some immersive technology tools are specific to a content area or objective, the resources in this book are adaptable to most classroom lessons. The activities in this chapter provide a general overview of some of the immersive tools and ideas for adapting them to student needs. The purpose of these activities is to gain a deeper insight into the tools and spark creative ways they can be used to engage our students.

Scavenger Hunts

There are many ways to use location-based messaging in education. The most commonly used way is a scavenger hunt. In a scavenger hunt, students search for items in a list—these can be objects or landmarks—and try to be the first to cross all of them off their list. There are many ways to tie scavenger hunt activities to learning and curricular goals. For example, hunts can tie in with a book the class is reading, a time period they are studying, or contain objects with certain scientific properties. With students who are beginning at a new school, scavenger hunts may be beneficial to cover various areas in the school and include rules and expectations. The tools described in this section can be used for scavenger hunts or other location-based activities.

WallaMe

The WallaMe app is a fairly new tool that uses augmented reality and location-based messaging. The app offers teachers a unique way to create a scavenger hunt by designing AR messages and leaving them in specific places for students to "discover." The messages can include typed text, drawings, stickers, and pictures. The student downloads the WallaMe mobile app on iOS or Google Play and searches for walls to view. When a student is in close enough proximity, the walls will be available to find and view (Figure 6.1). When the wall is found, the student can view the message and take a picture of the wall that is saved to their camera roll. Your wall can be private for a single individual, shared with a specific group of students, or open to the public to find and view.

Using the WallaMe app in the classroom is not limited to scavenger hunts. The teacher can leave notes, tips, activities, or other information floating around that students can capture every day. The students can create walls as a response exit ticket, or provide support for classmates on solving a problem. The WallaMe app can be a tool that parents use when visiting the classroom for Meet the Parents Day. Using the app to identify directions such as north, east, south, and west or solving math problems using nearby resources are ways the app can get students actively engaged and learning. The exciting element of discovering information makes the WallaMe app adaptable to any subject or grade level.

Figure 6.1

WallaMe app detecting a wall message.

The WallaMe app isn't intended for educational use only, so the rating is listed at ages 12 and up. The goal is to see these companies leading the way to create engaging activities that educators can adapt for the classroom.

Metaverse

The Metaverse app allows the educator to create multiple activities that include augmented and virtual reality. The students can engage in lessons that have a leader board to facilitate competition and challenge the students to work harder. The app uses GPS to provide activities to individuals who are in the correct location.

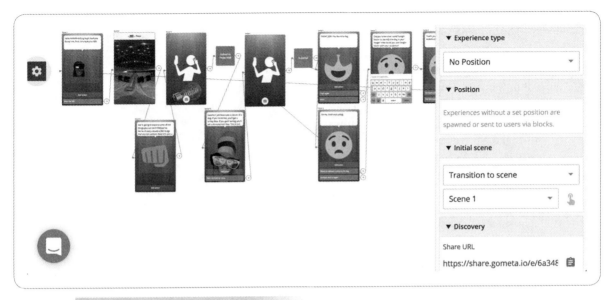

Figure 6.2

Metaverse Storyboard

The Metaverse app provides a storyboard, scenes, and blocks for educators to use to create experiences for their classroom (Figure 6.2). The website consists of several support videos to create content and provide a meaningful lessons for the students. The experience is shared by location, search, or shared by the educator with a permalink. The Metaverse app can be a basic lesson or made quite complex depending on the teacher's skills and needs for the lesson.

Some ways teachers can adapt Metaverse into their lessons are by:

- providing a personalized 360° virtual tour comporised of images and video;

- having students capture specific items in the scavenger hunt; or

- including assessment questions within the scavenger hunt.

The Metaverse app is a new concept for educators as it provides a way to create your own immersive technology experiences beyond the basics, but it has a significant learning curve when you first begin. As the application develops into an easier platform to create AR and VR experiences, I believe more of our classrooms will use it as an alternative to what is currently available in immersive technology apps.

Waypoint App

The Waypoint App has created an educational scavenger hunt using augmented reality. Educators can easily add questions that address lesson objectives, set the specific locations where the questions are hidden, and then have students hunt for questions following the map. The hunt is easily shared with students by airdrop, email, messages, or by sending the link in another platform.

The benefit of the Waypoint app is getting students get up and roam around the established boundaries set by the instructor to search for each question. The excitement of the hunt drives them to search for questions, solve them, and add coins to their treasure for solving the problem. While the Waypoint app requires newer iOS devices, the expansion to Android devices is coming. In addition, features such as uploading your own 3D objects will be part of the future updates.

Other Apps for Scavenger Hunts

Other educational apps that are beginning to use augmented and virtual reality with scavenger hunts are GeoGuessr, Gamar, and QuestUpon. These apps provide opportunities to engage in scavenger hunts while bringing in educational content. The apps are currently limited in content and availability to specific locations, however, the interest in augmented and virtual reality games is growing.

GeoGuessr uses 360° images from Google Streetview to explore an area. The object of the game is to identify your location with more precision than your opponents. The app categorizes a general location and the game sends the participant to multiple locations in that category. The game can be played on mobile devices and in a browser.

The **Gamar** app is mainly used for museums and universities. The benefit of this augmented reality scavenger hunt tool is the option to create your own experience. Although you can't share your custom hunts publicly without a paid subscription, students can engage in the hunt on the device it was created on.

The **QuestUpon** app has a great concept with interactive augmented reality games. The various quests take place in different parts of the world, so when the quest gets to a specific section, the user must be located in the correct spot to move on. As we see more scavenger hunt apps created, we will find that the exact location should not be required to engage in all the experiences.

Breakout EDU

Breakout EDU has become a popular game in education. It is driven by creativity, teamwork, and problem solving. The game provides a fun learning experience as it challenges students to compete in solving puzzles to win. The game centers around a series of questions. Each solved question results in unlocking the next part of the activity. As students work in groups, they compete against other groups to open all the locks first. The questions can be designed to challenge the students in all content areas and often the games include physical locks.

Although the physical locks are a fun way to see each question answered correctly, an alternative method to participate in Breakout EDU is in digital format—and with immersive technology, this becomes even more engaging for the participants. In fact, Breakout EDU can be an effective, hands-on way to introduce these tools. In this variation, players rotate through different stations, with each station consisting of questions to be solved. The questions are intended for a professional development training on augmented and virtual reality apps. The lesson uses devices instead of physical locks and the devices are set with unlock codes to open up the next experience. When you find the solution to each challenge, the answer to the solution is the unlock code on the next device.

Figure 6.3
Breakout EDU Techno Style game (tiny.cc/breakoutiste)

The unlock codes are single digit letters in this activity, however, the codes can be modified to fit multiple letters, numbers, or codes to solve the previous question. If the solution to the activity is the letter C, then "C" is the unlock code for the next device. If the team is unable to get the correct answer, they must go back and evaluate the question again. If the answer is correct, the code will unlock the next device and present the new challenge to solve. Each of the challenges features an AR or VR app for the classroom. Located at each station is a piece of paper describing the challenge and the tool. As groups visit each station, they have a sheet of paper to write down their solutions for a final activity. Here is an example of the challenges at each station.

In the first station, educators use the Google Translate app to translate text from Russian to English. The words in Russian are translated to say, "Two Letters After T." The educators will open the app, select the correct languages, and select the camera to view the words, which automatically translate into English. Only by using the augmented reality feature in the app can the educators know that the answer is the letter V. The unlock code on the device at the next station is "V," which the group will write on the solution sheet.

The next station features the RoundMe app, where you can view 360° images. Following the instructions, the educator will type in the search bar: "VIEW FROM THE TOP" and select the first 360° image available. The educator needs to identify where they are located (Eiffel Tower) in the 360° experience and write down the first letter of the location on the solution sheet. The educator will learn how to use the RoundMe app and use the unlock code "E" at the next station.

The third station uses the Quiver Vision app to show how a coloring page can come alive in augmented reality. The image shows an animal cell that, when viewed in the app, displays in AR the name of each of the parts. One of the parts is colored red and the educators will determine the last letter of its name. The last letter of the name is "I," which is the unlock code on the device in the next station.

The fourth station uses the CoSpaces app where the educator can type in the link and immediately get pulled into a 360° experience. The challenge is to identify the first letter of the color of the shirt warn by the man sitting down. The correct answer is white, which makes the unlock code "W" on the device at the next station.

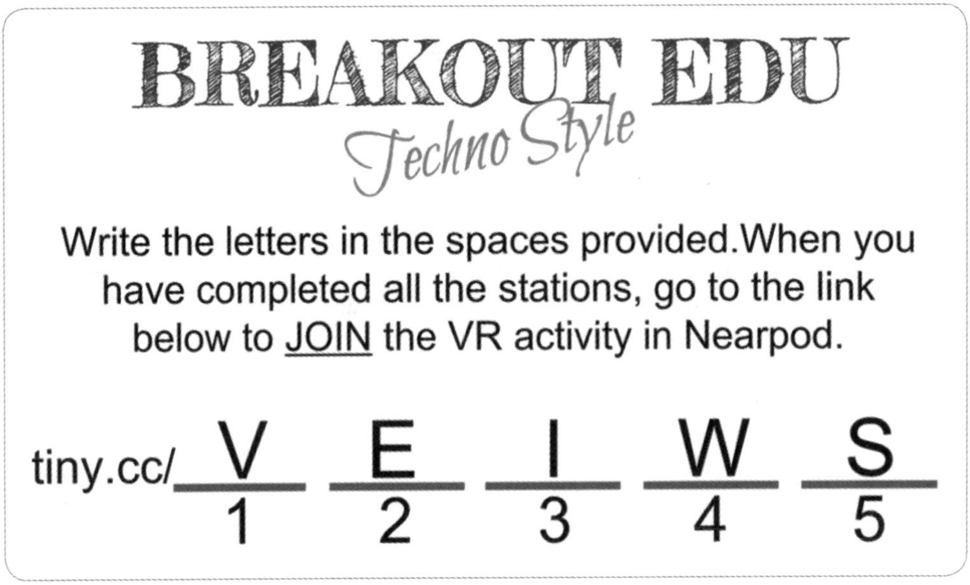

BREAKOUT EDU
Techno Style

Write the letters in the spaces provided. When you have completed all the stations, go to the link below to <u>JOIN</u> the VR activity in Nearpod.

tiny.cc/ <u>V</u> <u>E</u> <u>I</u> <u>W</u> <u>S</u>
     1   2   3   4   5

Figure 6.4

Breakout EDU Answer Sheet

The last station uses augmented reality to create a circuit board. The educators must identify the first letter of a critical piece on the board to solve the answer. The correct answer is the switch, making "S" the unlock code at the first station. The last station will rotate to the first station at the beginning.

When running this activity, I have the educators start at any station and rotate the groups every five minutes. The answer sheet (shown in Figure 6.4) has all the unlock answers from the stations, which reveal the link to the final Nearpod activity. By creating a shortened link in tiny.cc, the game can be adjusted when changes are made. Creating a Breakout EDU game can be simple or extensive depending on how complicated or customized you want to make the challenges. Many challenges can be found at the breakoutedu.com website and can be filtered by grade and subject level.

Exploratory Play with Cubes and Blocks

Using the simple concept of playing with blocks, developers have come up with a way to incorporate play with immersive technology. Using cubes that have six faces, each of the faces features a trigger image to scan for augmented reality. In many cases, combining cubes together to create a new trigger image brings the most interaction and engagement. Each of the cube resources function differently to provide multiple learning activities at various grade levels.

Some of the cube activities involve building with blocks, similar to Minecraft. The apps use a trigger image to identify where to layer the blocks using the device camera. Building with 3D blocks in our world is much more realistic than in a virtual world. The following apps include interactive learning experiences that feature construction and provide multiple learning opportunities for students.

EON Experience

Although the EON Creator app has many augmented and virtual reality lessons, the free EON Experience app includes an activity to build with blocks using the EON trigger image. Students can scan the EON trigger image and keep it in the camera view in the app while they build on a block similar to Minecraft. The opportunities to explain gravity, reactions, environments, or many other topics are endless when giving your students the chance to show their knowledge the same way they prefer to play.

The best part of the experience is that the app remembers what was created so the structures can continue to grow and develop throughout time. Other than a traditional video game, it's rare to find an activity that remembers what was already built and this is especially true within augmented reality. EON Experience is currently building multiplayer options to allow multiple students to build in the same space at the same time using augmented reality.

World Builder enables our students to become architects to create unlimited structures using blocks. The benefit of the app is the ease of use as it identifies the EON trigger image and immediately provides the building blocks to design a structure. Using World Builder in the EON Experience, students can design structures using various architectural styles that match available materials, fashions, beliefs, technology, weather conditions, and regional characteristics. The building projects can demonstrate knowledge of cultures and history. Providing a platform for students to build using augmented reality allows students to show knowledge in a non-traditional format and demonstrate a much deeper understanding.

Try It! Build Something in EON

To begin using World Builder, download the EON Experience app from iOS at **tiny. cc/eoncreatorapple** or Google Play at **tiny.cc/eoncreatorandroid** and open the World Builder activity under Edutainment. You will need the EON trigger image found in the EON lesson plans in the previous chapter or on the EON Reality website at **eonreality.com/eevr**. While looking at the trigger image through the camera in the app, the options to build a structure appear around the corners of the screen. Select the material for the structure by touching the spinning cube and then place the plus sign in the middle at the location where you want to add the cube. Select the large button with the hand to place the cube in that spot.

ArCraft

Building games are popular with students mainly because they offer creativity. The blocks are versatile enough to make just about anything, and students seem to enjoy the challenge of undertaking the most difficult builds. ArCraft takes the concept of building within a 360° environment and places the building on top of your own trigger image using augmented reality.

When starting ArCraft, the app will show the options to play or load a game. When selecting load, the game will load any previous builds made in the app. Again, this preservation of previous work is another great and rare feature. If play is selected in the app, a new build will begin. The first requirement to start a new build or load a previous build is selecting an appropriate trigger image. A quick reminder, trigger images are best when they feature high contrasting colors and are scanned in good lighting. When the proper trigger image is selected, the building can begin. The trigger image can be different each time you come back to the app to build.

Similar to Minecraft, the blocks vary as they have different purposes. However, the ArCraft app uses different blocks to create a theme for your build rather than to distinguish functionality. The blocks are found in the chest, called the "sandbox" and resemble grass, dirt, brick, wood, water, and more. These blocks can build structures, animals, plants, and just about anything else. Showing knowledge through 3D objects makes the learning more fun, relevant to student interest, and is flexible with any content or grade level. An elementary student can build a structure that measures a specific width and height, while a secondary student may design a functioning house that conforms to a specific surface area.

AR Circuits

The AR Circuits app brings together fun and learning by exploring the basic concepts of circuits and electricity. No electronics kit in your classroom? No problem. The AR Circuits app brings the experience through your mobile screen using augmented reality. The app has a small cost to download in both the Google Play and App Store but is well worth the price. The printable trigger image cards have symbols to represent components. Each card serves a different purpose to make working electric components. When viewing the trigger image cards within the AR Circuits app, the cards turn into realistic simulated components.

As the cards are rearranged, the activity builds knowledge about various components including the wire, battery, switch, bulbs, resistor, and conductor (Figure 6.5). The various parts can be placed together to turn on a bulb using the right components. The user can dim the bulb by adjusting the resistance and the battery voltage.

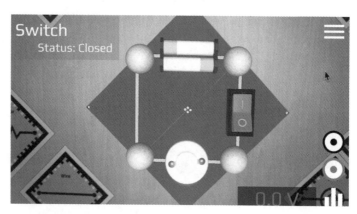

Figure 6.5

AR Circuits App

In addition to exploring the cards, the exploratory play within the app builds knowledge about each of the components. When a required component is missing, it's clear that the bulb is not receiving electricity. The activities allow the user to receive immediate feedback by testing out the various combinations of components and seeing the results. The combinations are seen through the mobile device in augmented reality and either present no light, a dim light, or a fully lit light.

One of the main reasons AR Circuits is so fun is because it requires problem solving. The mystery of finding out how to turn on the light is just the beginning. Determining how many lights a battery can power or what happens when adding resistance were some of the explorations I went on when first playing with the app. Having no background with circuits, I jumped at the opportunity to learn in a safe environment without feeling foolish if I didn't know the answer or chose incorrect combinations. In addition, I didn't have to buy a kit or find the tools to create light.

The AR Circuits app provides the learning without the worry of the dangers such as broken bulbs and burns.

The flexibility to explore the app on paper was helpful but printing out the trigger image cards may not always be an option. The virtual cards are a convenient way to explore the app with all the components available. The cards easily align against one another without overlapping. I found it difficult to line up the paper cards as they can easily slide on top of each other.

One of the ways to align the trigger image cards more easily is by printing out the cards on a net that folds up to cubes similar to the 4D Elements. The cubes make it easy to align the components without the pieces of paper sliding on top of one another. The option to print out cards with or without the names of the components is available as well as printing out the cards on a cube. The app also provides a virtual voltmeter to determine the electric potential. When two components are connected, the voltmeter can determine the voltage by selecting the junction where they meet.

Merge Cube

The Merge Cube (previously called the Holocube) is an appealing choice for educators, who are snatching up the reasonably-priced accessories to use in the classroom, and for good reason. What's not to like about a hologram you can hold in your hand? These six-sided, lightweight cubes are covered on each side with glyphs that transform into lifelike AR and VR images when viewed through a device or headset. Retailing at $14.99 or less at the time of this printing, the cubes are a great, hands-on way to get started with immersive technology.

Figure 6.6

Merge Cube Galactic Explorer

While augmented reality features in a cube have been around for a few years, Merge Cube takes a different approach as a distributor of apps and games developed by others. The apps are shared by the MergeVR company, but the developers create the apps for the cube and individual purchases are made based on the developer's price. Many of the Merge Cube apps are free to download and test out.

The apps use both augmented and virtual reality for activities using the cube. MergeVR also sells a headset with the camera exposed that works perfectly with the software and provides the full experience. Both the viewer and the cube are made of a foam material, making it easy to clean and safe to use without worry of breaking. The viewer adds an additional layer of protection to the device while holding the cube in your hand.

Here are a few apps to try out with the Merge Cube.

The Th!ngs app is the best Merge Cube app to begin exploring the features of the cube. The app provides an assortment of experiences—from holding a fire in your hand to flying through the universe in a space ship. Using both augmented and virtual reality, the cube brings hours of entertainment to a wide range of ages and interests. The Th!ngs app is a great way to get a sample of the Merge Cube's capabilities.

One of the apps that I found to be interesting for education is the building app **Dig It**. Similar to Minecraft but building on or into the cube instead of in a device screen, the app allows the user to customize the cube by adding blocks. Some of the resources include stone, sand, grass, brick, and lava. The difference between the Dig It app and others is the ability to see the cube in augmented reality with little interruption. The cube has great contrasting color to give a seamless adventure. The toolbox gives the user a chance to select a variety of resources while the build mode allows the you to add or take away blocks. The world setting opens the door to saved world or worlds that other builders have created and that are available to download. Beginning with another world can get the user more familiar with the tools and options in the app before starting their own build.

Another educational Merge Cube app is **Galactic Explorer**, where students can explore our solar system in the palms of their hands. The app has a small cost to download in both the Google Play and App Store. While viewing the planets in orbit around the sun, users can select each planet to see a list of interesting facts about it. Viewing the planets from every angle may be exactly what a student will need to gain understanding about the solar system.

A storytelling app called **57° North** by Mighty Coconut provides the students a chance to explore a story with multiple variations as you "choose your path." As the story comes alive inside of the cube, the plot will pause and offer options to progress through the story. The students can choose their preferences by rotating the cube in the direction of their choice. The Mighty Coconut company has combined storytelling and AR in this delightful app, which is available for a small cost.

The **Dino Digger** app takes the experience of augmented reality in the cube and adds interaction. The students will become paleontologists and dig for fossils using various tools. As the bones are discovered, the student can add them to the museum to admire and learn about the dinosaur, all from inside the cube. The purposeful activities that combine AR, interaction, and learning are well executed in this app.

Want to test the experience of using a Merge Cube to see how it might work with your classroom? You can download and construct a paper version that will work with your mobile device. Instructions are available here: **tinyurl.com/y9r29jto**.

Virtual Field Trips

Virtual field trips are one of the prime categories driving the popularity of virtual reality in the classroom. These types of field trips go beyond a digital experience to a virtual reality experience by giving a 360° view. The field trips give our students access to lead their own tour as they direct which location to explore. Students can spend the amount of time they need to discover new areas, artifacts, cultures, and more.

Student standards continue to emphasize global citizenship. As our students are required to have more connections around the world, we often look for these connections through video chats. A live video chat is one option to build global connections, but we must begin with building global knowledge to avoid offensive comments or propagating inaccurate facts. Preparing for international collaboration should include providing background for your students on the geography and culture of the students they will be interacting with. A virtual field trip can provide perspective, cultural sensitivity, and relatable conversations.

Allowing our students to explore anywhere in the world has many advantages. We are able to use virtual field trips to bring our students to impossible places such as a different time era, inside the cell of a living creature, or into an active volcano. These adventures can add depth to our lesson plans and replace or enhance pictures inside of a textbook. As students have more engagement with virtual field trips in their learning, there is a greater opportunity to deepen meaning, relevance, and retention.

Google Earth

Google Earth has been around for some time. What began as a website became an app and most recently added the benefits of 3D and 360° views. Exploring the world through satellite imagery is fascinating to reveal remote destinations and capture moments in history. To use Google Earth, use the Chrome browser and open **earth.google.com** or download the app in the Google Play or App Store. If you have an HTC Vive or an Oculus Rift, you have access to Google Earth VR. I anticipate the VR features will spread to other platforms in the future as more browsers adopt virtual reality.

> The students in Tracy Mercier's classroom at CREC International Magnet School of Connecticut enjoyed using immersive technology to learn. The kindergarteners explained they love to travel to different places through Google Maps. The students were able to visit a recycling center and were absolutely amazed with the experience. "The fifth-grade group were able to relive the revolutionary war and were able to travel back to colonial America to see where general Washington stayed during the war." (Mercier, 2017).

VOYAGER   The most recent release of Google Earth has the Voyager feature. These interactive stories bring current and past events to life as they share 3D views, videos, and information cards. One of the highlights of Voyager is the hurricane Harvey experience that gives a full picture of the devastation that hit the southern portions of Texas with massive flooding in 2017. Describing the facts of the hurricane, Google Earth walks the viewer through numerous locations that had significant damage.

Through Voyager, the students can become explorers with Lewis and Clark, Marco Polo, and Eric the Red. Students can follow the journeys of Charles Dickens and Ernest Hemingway. In addition to these historical explorations, the locations you can visit are almost endless, offering travel to national parks, global beaches, stadiums, craters, and much more.

FEEL LUCKY?   Another feature included in Google Earth is the "I'm Feeling Lucky" tab. What an exhilarating experience to jump to an unknown location in the world that takes your breath away. Google selects a surprise location and shares new facts through a visual journey to that location. Imagine the places your students can explore every day while building global knowledge.

USA Today VR Stories

The USA Today VR Stories app has developed a powerful way to communicate using virtual reality. Bringing together relevant news stories and expanding them into a virtual, 360° setting is a brilliant to share experiences along with information. Students can engage in the latest news while being brought to those locations. The virtual reality experience is found in the USA Today app in the Google Play or App Store. The 360° stories can be found on the USA Today YouTube channel. One of the benefits of this resource is the access to the content on mobile devices and computers as an alternative to the app.

Storytelling in virtual reality is essentially what we are experiencing in VR Stories. One of the stories I watched was called the "Extraordinary Gator Feeding Frenzy in 360°." If you need an activity for a lesson on carnivores, you will want to check this story out. The story shows how Jim Darlington, the curator of reptiles at Saint Augustine Alligator Farm Zoological Park in Florida, finds his place among hungry alligators. The footage of the feeding frenzy is incredible.

Taking a step back into Medieval times, VR Stories does a great job of describing the sport of jousting. You'll learn all the strategies involved with the sport and how each move can potentially create a dangerous situation, including the point of contact in the competition, which can be intense. The actors describing life in simpler times is engaging and informative.

Another historical story that can offer an immersive experience is the reenactment of Pearl Harbor. Climbing inside of the virtual submarine was uncomfortable and I immediately felt claustrophobic. These historical stories bring our students into the events, where they are more likely to be engaged than just by hearing or reading about them.

Discovery VR

A similar resource to VR Stories is the Discovery VR app. This app brings many of the Discovery television shows into a 360° experience. Some of the most fascinating videos include the Discovery VR Atlas, where you'll be immersed into cultures and experiences around the world. The DNews Labs explore practical uses of science as it's found in the world around us. The science and technology resources are integrated throughout the app. Be advised, however, there are many 360° videos that are unrelated to education, so you'll want to explore the site before unleashing students on it.

RoundMe

The RoundMe site offers a variety of ways to explore 360° experiences. The original team was determined to use 360° photography for real estate and had a difficult time finding a place to upload these images. The site offers a way to explore beautiful immersive experiences. Although the views are breathtaking, the additional content with the locations make this resource a fantastic and easy way to use virtual reality with your students.

There are several ways to explore experiences inside of RoundMe. A simple way to get familiar with the website is through the Explore tab, which gives you the top picks from the editors, new uploads, and the collections. The collections tab brings an assortment of common themed 360° images together in a virtual reality scene. The recent and top picks tab is constantly changing to feature new uploads and the search bar allows students to match places with their interests.

In addition, the option to search for 360° images and collections can be found in the world map view. The map view is easy to navigate as you click and drag on the page to find a specific location of images. Viewing the images through the map gives perspective on the geographical features in various regions. Students can explore regions and gather connections or identify specific architectural features prior to engaging in a new lesson.

Learning Transported Challenge

Using exploratory cubes, show how you've transformed your classroom with play.

Customize your own scavenger hunt or breakout activity for your students. Share your resources for others to adapt for their classroom.

Explore how you might use a virtual field trip or one of the Google Earth tools in a content area lesson. Share your ideas with the #ARVRinEdu community and get input.

7 From Experience to Creation

M any classroom immersive technology resources begin with consumption of content. Our students have an enormous amount of resources available for using technology and we should ensure that students not only absorb content in the classroom, but create it as well. As students become familiar and comfortable with the technology, they should be encouraged and guided to shift from intake of content to creation of content.

Creating content has advantages for our students and gives the flexibility to adapt to specific needs rather than waiting on a tool to be created. One of the benefits of being a content creator is the pride and satisfaction that comes from having the vision to go beyond what others have done before. Using tools to begin creating immersive technology content can easily lead to students forming groundbreaking new resources. The creative, problem-solving skills students need should be practiced regularly in the classroom. Immersive technology is no different from any other media in that regard and it extends more freedom to design for a future of learning that has yet to exist.

The progression of immersive technology is changing so rapidly that it can feel overwhelming. The corollary to this is that overwhelming pace also brings better, easier, and more powerful capabilities. We've recently witnessed an influx of easy AR, VR, and MR creation tools that are flexible for any subject or grade level. The flexibility of the tool determines how widespread immersive technology will integrate into the curriculum. The ease of use of the tool will drive its adoption across all skill levels.

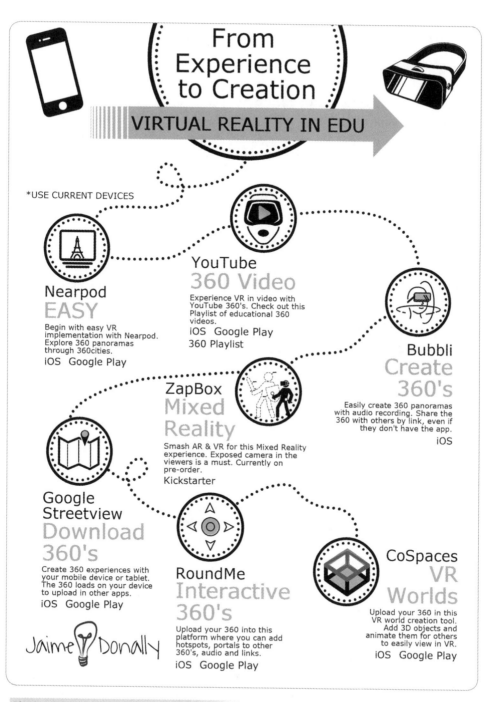

Figure 7.1

Virtual Reality Experience to Creation

Living in 360°

Figure 7.1 should help illustrate approaches to building the necessary skills for students to bein developing virtual reality content. The resources don't require a large device purchase or extensive knowledge. Most of the tools can be used by students without any training at all. Although the resources shared here are intended to get students and teachers started, there are many other apps that are similar in concept, and of course, there are always new tools being released.

Nearpod and YouTube

Mainly due to the ease of use, my first recommended tool to experience virtual reality creation is Nearpod. In Nearpod, it's easy to search for 360° images within the content area and journey on virtual field trips. The tool can be adapted to meet the needs of any classroom. Going on a VR adventure in Nearpod is as simple as typing the place you're ready to go.

The 360° images search feature in Nearpod is a subscription-based product, although many of the other features are free. The app uses the library in 360cities which offers virtual experiences that you can add to a lesson. Having a paid Nearpod subscription is priceless when it comes to easy 360° implementations. One of the original pioneers for Nearpod, Steve Bambury, Head of Digital Learning and Innovation at JESS Dubai, used Nearpod to create virtual tours to the tallest building in the world, Mars, and even the tomb of Rameses in ancient Egypt. You can explore these lessons on his website at **tiny.cc/stevenearpod**.

I've presented numerous Nearpod trainings to large and small groups and one thing I can always depend on is the consistency. Having a large group participate in virtual reality at the same time is typically a disaster because of the bandwidth demand. However, when I share Nearpod, I find that 200 attendees can run the experience at the same time without a problem.

When determining how to use Nearpod, you can present the lesson on multiple platforms. I always recommend using a mobile device in the app for the most immersive experience, however, your students can also load the lesson on computers using a browser. Nearpod is also located in the Chrome App Store to give students the best experience on Chromebooks. The more flexibility with the platform, the more likely our classrooms can adapt the resource. Nearpod has found a way to adapt to many classroom needs and configurations with simple VR lessons.

Another resource to find 360° content is YouTube. The ability to upload 360° videos to YouTube was a complete game changer for the future of videos. You may have never seen a tornado in your lifetime, but using YouTube, you can watch a storm chaser follow a tornado as it throws debris onto the roads. The power of an immersive experience is the real reason 360° videos can change how we learn, especially in situations where we couldn't experience something in real life.

Finding educational resources on YouTube can be a challenge, especially when it relates to 360° content. You can access my collection of 360° educational videos on my YouTube playlist **ARVRinEDU**, where dozens of virtual reality videos are available to use with multiple content areas and grade levels. The playlist is updated regularly but feel free to start your own playlist by adding 360° videos that relate to your classroom.

You are not limited to the content availalble on Nearpod or YouTube. You can upload your own content to either. Nearpod allows uploads of images, videos, slides, and more. Creating an account in Nearpod is free and there are no limits to how many images or videos you can upload. Not all uploads are accepted for public view, but you can add your 360° images into a lesson by copying the URL in 360cities and pasting it into a web content slide in Nearpod.

You can upload 360° videos in YouTube if you have access to a 360° camera. The price of these cameras has continued to drop, making them much more affordable. In addition to uploading 360° videos, streaming video in YouTube Live and Periscope are now using VR. As 360° cameras become more widespread, more live video platforms will include VR livestreaming in their platforms.

Create 360° Experiences

An enormous amount of software and resources are available for creating immersive experiences. Many require prior knowledge and coding skills and the huge library of tools on the web and mobile apps can easily mask the simple tools that are available. Fortunately, the list of appropriate and easy creation tools continues to grow as it increases in popularity. The options that follow have proven themselves useful for education and have withstood the test of time.

Streetview

The Google Streetview app is by far the most widely used 360° creation app in education. It maintains a simple way to create the 360° images with an advanced stitching software program that produces incredible images. One of the most important features in Google Streetview is the option to keep the image on the device. Students in early elementary can grasp the concept of creating 360° images with the simple tutorials and visuals to guide you through the process.

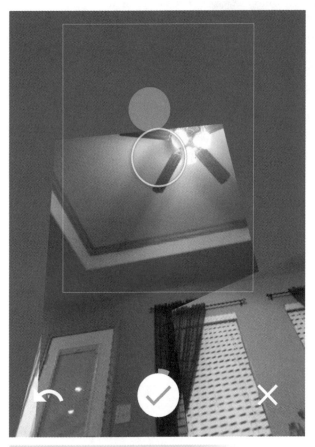

Figure 7.2

360° Image Taken in Google Streetview

The skill of capturing good 360° images takes time and practice. Here are some tips to help you get started.

Use a Tripod or Location Guide

Many people rotate the device around their body to take each photo, however when you do this, the camera actually travels in a circle and at times will be a distance away from the original position. The distance between the starting and ending locations can create odd stitching from one photo to the next and warp some of the images. A better option is for the person to rotate around the device while keeping the device in the same location as it spins. A tripod can work well, but using a guide to keep the image in a similar place as it rotates around is a better option. A good recommendation is hanging a weight on a wire from the bottom of the device to help you keep its location consistent as you rotate around it.

Follow an Order when Stitching Photos

Another recommendation for good photo stitching is taking pictures in a vertical line before rotating horizontally. Take a photo in the center and then above and below that image before rotating to the left or to the right. Stitching software can better determine the photo edges when the sequence is done in this order.

Many other apps are available to capture 360° images, but not all have the option to keep the image in the camera roll of the device. Hosting 360° images on a website is beneficial in many cases, but having the flexibility to use that same 360° image in other apps is ideal. When the image is stored on the device, you have access to the highest quality of those stitched photos. When uploading a 360° image or video into a website, the sites generally recommend a minimum resolution to ensure a high-quality experience. Giving our students a tool to store the best quality for future applications will extend our projects into new technologies as standards rise.

When the 360° image is complete in Google Streetview, you'll select the green circle at the bottom (Figure 7.2), and the image will be loaded onto the camera roll of your device. Should you want to share the experience by link, the 360° images must be published in Google Maps. Students can feel the experience is more authentic because they become contributors of content for Google. By contributing content, others can see their creative work and students can also get feedback and see some of the data on how well their experience performs.

RoundMe

The RoundMe site does a great job of making your 360° images interactive. Initially, I looked at ways to use RoundMe for virtual field trips, but the website has much more to offer when uploading and publishing 360° images. The free account allows for 15 uploads a month, which is more than enough for the average user. In addition to the site, RoundMe has an app that gives you access to adjust your images, add interactions, and view experiences in the VR view.

When loading a 360° image, there are options to add interactive features. The first option is adding hotspots that are set to a specific location on top of the 360° image. In the hotspot, you can add a title and description to detail what is in the image. Hotspots are also useful for identifying people, landmarks, vocabulary definitions, and more—any information you want to include can be layered on top of your image. Interactive objects are hidden or revealed by tapping the screen. To add the hotspot, you can click and drag the exclamation mark where you want it placed in the image. Type the desired text in the title and description of the hotspot when the image is in editing mode.

The hotspots aren't limited by text, but can also include images and links. Allowing students to further explore a concept that they see inside of a VR experience extends the learning opportunity. Expand the possibilities of virtual field trips by linking a quiz from Google Classroom or adding a game from a website. More importantly, giving students the chance to create their own virtual tours. Students can create their own 360° images and add what they've learned within the experience for a deeper way to demonstrate knowledge.

Another important feature in RoundMe is the option to connect multiple 360° experiences by using portals. By selecting the floating bubbles, students can jump from one experience to another without interruption. RoundMe created the use of portals to provide virtual tours. Our students can easily join and create these tours using their own 360° images.

Directional sound is a powerful addition to VR experiences that delivers a more immersive experience for the user. Adding directions in the tour or giving important information about the scene are ways to use directional sound. As the student rotates around the virtual space, the sound will get louder or softer depending on which direction they look. Consider including music by selecting an audio file from your computer and loading it into the experience. The option to adjust the degree that the sounds reaches is an added bonus. The sound can be located in a very specific spot, extending only 30 degrees, or it can extend in the full 360°.

The map feature in RoundMe gives the user a sense of where they are located based on the surrounding places. The map will show the scene though a Google Earth view. Both of the views can support learning with the VR field trip experience. The students can make predictions on where they believe they landed and then check how close their predictions were in the map view. The RoundMe map feature can support learning by deepening the students' sense of direction and ability to read a map and explore geographical content.

To get a glimpse of your 360° experience, create a snapshot of the best view in the scene. Students will arrive facing the same direction of the snapshot when first entering the experience. Adding portals of other 360° images will have the snapshot image in the bubble as the students are exploring. The snapshot is an optional feature, but using it can entice students to open new portals or can simply enhance the experience by highlighting the best view.

CoSpaces

CoSpaces is both a website and an app for creating VR worlds. There are many fantastic tools in the platform that mark CoSpaces as one of the top resources for students to use to create virtual reality experiences.

The platform is simple to use. 3D objects are dragged and dropped into a 360° space. Once created, the space is easily shared using a link, social media, or QR code. The viewer can open the link, which is redirected to open in the CoSpaces

Figure 7.3

Animated CoSpaces Scene

app. CoSpaces has always been free, and recently they've also added a premium plan specifically for classrooms called CoSpaces EDU.

Access to the many 3D objects available in CoSpaces is useful for building multiple scenes, but students can also add their own items to the space. Loading your own audio or images provides the freedom to create a personalized space. The upload feature will also search for images in Bing that you can include in the space.

Using the building blocks in CoSpaces, you have access to more than the library of 3D objects. The building blocks are adjustable and can change in color, proportion, and scale, making the virtual worlds able to demonstrate any content. Making changes to each block is easily done on either the computer or mobile device.

In addition to building virtual worlds, CoSpaces includes a coding feature for the 3D objects using Blockly. Students are no longer just creating still objects, but have the opportunity to animate them using code. Having no experience in coding in the past, I found using the Blockly feature in CoSpaces to be exploratory and fun. The platform is simple enough for early elementary, but offers advanced options using script that can challenge students as they become more proficient.

There are ten environments to choose from to enhance the experience. The environments are wrapped around the scene. CoSpaces is a fantastic tool to load your 360° images, because of the many additional interactions that you can add to the scene. Uploading your own 360-degree environment, adding 3D objects on top of that 360° image and animating those objects using code is beyond impressive.

An easy way to add animation is by adding characters to your scene. You can easily select your characters and the animation you want to show. In this scene, there are emotions added to the characters using animation. I uploaded images to a layer on the screen and used the audio from my Ignite session at ISTE 2017 (Figure 7.3). You can view the experience at **cospac.es/Kntp** using the CoSpaces app or your computer browser.

3D Creation to AR

If educators have heard of augmented reality in the past, it's typically because they've run across Aurasma at some point. The Aurasma app is quite popular for creating AR experiences because of its simplicity. But perhaps its biggest advantage is that it's available for mobile devices. There are numerous resources for experiences using augmented reality on a mobile device, but few of those resources include creation tools for students.

The following are a few tools to move from experiencing augmented reality to creating your own AR. Most of the apps are available in the Google Play and iTunes app store and the studios are located in a browser.

Creation Tools

- Spin Magic (**tiny.cc/spinmagicapple**) Draw and animate in 3D.
- MSQRD (**tiny.cc/msqrdapple** and **tiny.cc/msqrdandroid**) Design AR filters.
- Storyfab (**tiny.cc/storyfabapple**) Create AR stories.

Creation Studios

- HP Reveal, formerly Aurasma Studio (**studio.hpreveal.com/landing**) The easy to use interface of this AR creation tool allows users to quickly generate auras for augmented reality experiences.

- Zapworks Studio (**zap.works**) Offering three different tools for AR creation—widgets, designer, and studio, this platform allows users to create interactive experiences that can be accessed with a zapcode.

- Blippbuilder (**web.blippar.com/blipp-builder**) User-friendly AR creation platform that includes options for those with and without coding experience.

Virtual Reality Experience to Creation with 3DC

The most impressive immersive technology experiences include viewing and interacting with 3D objects. Creating 3D objects can be simple using apps designed for beginners. The 3DC app (3DC stands for 3D Creationist) is a multiplatform tool that can be found in the Google Play Store, App Store, and in your browser at **3dc.io**. In addition to the app, 3DC is available as a Chrome extension for Chromebooks.

3DC makes creating 3D objects easy as you mold a shape that can be formed into anything imaginable. Starting with a basic cube, you can stretch, drag around, and rotate the objects to transform them into something new. Some of the basic shapes to use for building include pyramid, prism, sphere, cylinder, and cone. The objects are placed on a stage area that can be shifted around and viewed in 360° so you can see the objects from every angle.

The drawing tool is a feature that allows 3D creation for all ages. Students can use the tool to easily create any object. Although colors can be adjusted for each object, a limited number of textures are available within the app. The pro (paid) account provides many more textures plus the ability to upload your own images to use as textures.

3DC also offers the ability to create 3D text. To include text, students can type words into the stage area and have them rendered as 3D objects. Students can combine their objects with descriptive words or titles.

When the 3D object is complete, the simple save and export option in 3DC provides all the needed formats for sharing student creations. The tool makes adding 3D objects into other platforms easy with exports in OBJ and STL formats. These formats are the same common formats acceptable by most 3D printing software.

A few projects that students could use with 3DC are:

- Designing objects for 3D printing

- Generating models to demonstrate knowledge

- Building structures
- Creating a demo of a product
- Presenting a concept to solve a problem, and much more.

Giving our students a 3D stage to house their created products is necessary for the skills they'll need tomorrow. As immersive technology becomes more interwoven in education, our students will need to take their skills in 3D design and include them for future augmented and virtual reality experiences.

Scan 3D Objects with Qlone

Designing objects from the beginning is a fantastic way to create simple 3D designs, however, there are times when more detail is needed in the object. An app that uses your iOS device to scan 3D objects is Qlone. The Qlone app (pronounced clone), is taking the concept of 3D design and making it simple to scan an object and export the object into another platform.

Using a QR code printed on a mat, an object is placed on the mat and the iOS device scans around the object. The best scan is done when rotating the mat in circles while holding the device in the same place. As the object is scanned from every angle, it loads in the app, ready to be exported to another platform.

Another feature in Qlone is the option to view the scanned objects in augmented reality by selecting AR and viewing the printed mat. The object can be adjusted after a scan to change or add color, create a blurred effect, and to cut off any unnecessary parts.

The export file types vary and some of the options are free while others require a small fee. The free options include creating an image file, a GIF that rotates your object around, and exporting to Sketchfab, Shapeway, and i-Materialise. After exporting your 3D image, you can view it through a device in augmented or virtual reality. The export formats that require a fee are OBJ, STL, X3D, and PLY, which are the file types that work with 3D printing.

Sending the scanned object to Sketchfab makes the object viewable from all angles by providing a link to the object. In addition, Sketchfab makes the object viewable in virtual and augmented reality. The properties can be set to state where the viewer will look at the object and the distance from the object when viewing it in AR and VR. In addition, the environment for the object can be modified to give a more realistic experience.

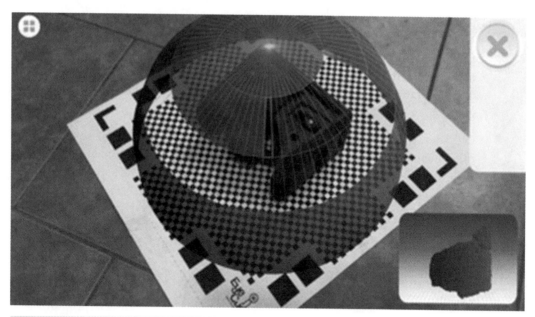

Figure 7.4

Qlone scanning 3D objects

View 3D Objects in DottyAR

The DottyAR resource brings 3D created objects to viewers by layering them in augmented reality. The resource is available in your browser at **dottyar.com** and in the Google Play and App Store. When you upload 3D objects into DottyAR, the site generates a shortened link and QR code so you can easily share your object with others. The free site allows you to upload ten 3D models at a time. A subscription is required to add more.

After loading the 3D object, you can share the QR code and shortened link by selecting "more" on the homepage. The installed DottyAR app is required to scan the QR code and reveal the 3D object. Another option to share the object is typing in a four-letter code. After scanning or typing in the code, the object appears, layered on top of your reality through the camera and rotated to fit any location. The option to snap the 3D object to another trigger image is available within the app, making it easier to connect the object to relevant content.

A fantastic way to share your 3D object is using the collaboration feature. Students can share the collaboration code with others to view the 3D objects together and can view it from many angles while sharing their impressions of the object. In addition, a collaboration window opens to begin a chat discussion. As the group is in collaboration mode, the owner can load other objects and keep the conversation going.

Our students continue to build their portfolio of designs. Providing a way to display those items is important. The DottyAR app provides a place for students to share their 3D created objects by sharing it with augmented reality. As more apps provide a platform, flexibility will be the key to success when using 3D creations in augmented reality.

Learning Transported Challenge

Ask your students to solve a problem by building and presenting a 3D object. Display the 3D object using augmented reality in DottyAR.

Have your students create a classroom virtual field trip by creating, uploading, and sharing 360° images.

8 Storytelling

Traditional storytelling involves a reader or a listener who uses their imagination to piece together what is read in the story. With its ability to create experiences and bring words and pictures to life, it's obvious that immersive technology will also influence the books we read. The world has made major shifts in how content is delivered in the past few decades, but somehow, the only change we've seen in classroom textbooks has been the conversion from print to digital.

Some publishers have begun to incorporate augmented reality by turning the pages of their books into trigger images. Each app runs the experience that's connected to a specific book. One of the challenges teachers face with augmented reality books is finding which books include augmented reality experiences. The following books are some of the examples that include AR interactions and that are appropriate for the classroom.

Bugs 3D

The *Bugs 3D* book was created with a series of other augmented reality books by Popar. The book contains images and information about various insects. The interactions in this book include animated environments and habitats, 360° views, video descriptions, realistic sounds, and the ability to take a picture or record a video within the app.

The Bugs 3D adventures begin by purchasing the book by Popar and downloading the app in the Google Play or App Store. The app will confirm the purchase of the book by scanning a page to open the options to interact with the content in augmented and virtual reality. The app will walk the user through the various options in the book and then open the camera view. Scan the front cover and each of the pages to begin. The book includes three different modes: Book Mode, Card Mode, and VR Mode.

Book Mode uses the camera to view the insect in 3D and provides information about the insect that's found in the book. The student can watch a video about the insect and view and identify its body parts. The book mode also gives you the control to walk the insect around in your own environment using augmented reality.

Card Mode uses the pages of cards found in the back of the book. Each card represents a different insect and, when scanned in the app, displays a 3D animated version of the insect on top of the QR code. The insect can be viewed and manipulated to change size and direction based on your interest as you keep the QR code in view. You can access more information about the insect by tapping the image on the screen.

VR Mode will shrink you down to the size of an ant so you can experience each insect from a bug's eye view. The screen includes a joystick to look around the space or uses the gyroscope to view the scenes by rotating the device around. Look around the scene in 360° to see each insect interact within their habitat. Tap the screen where an insect is located to learn more about it.

Using multiple learning styles, students can explore each insect using AR and VR. This type of interaction presents a personalized learning opportunity by allowing students to explore their individual areas of interest in the most effective way for each student. The animated environments and specimens make the learning more realistic and engaging.

Anomaly

Anomaly is a 370-page graphic novel intended for young adult readers. This science fiction and fantasy book is full of incredible graphics that display our world in the year 2717. In the story, the world is nearly depleted of resources, forcing humans to live in isolated cities or to orbit the earth in a space station.

The story has vivid imagery on every page and the associated Anomaly Ultimate Augmented Reality app includes presents the images in 3D. The app is found in both the Google Play and App Store. On certain pages, additional interactions are available to gain the backstory of the characters. As the pages show more characters, the app uses the camera to scan the page and reveal a deeper insight into the character's connection to the story.

Using AR, the reader can see the characters appear in their space. When viewing the 3D character, they can select the arrow at the bottom of the screen to get extensive knowledge about the character's physical traits, offensive and defensive capabilities, and exploitable attributes.

An alternative app associated with the story is the Anomaly Comic Con app. The app is used to demonstrate Anomaly at conferences and to view various posters and cards associated with the story. One feature in the Comic Con app that is different than the book app is face swap. Your device camera is used so that you become the character by layering the facial characteristic on top of your own.

Anomaly can get our most resistant students interested in reading and learning by using immersive technology. This graphic novel brings augmented reality to our secondary students through story, interaction, and impressive visuals.

Spy Quest

Spy Quest, a new augmented reality book series, is coming from Scotland to the United States. The SpyQuest app allows you to scan the images within the book that then become a video on top of the page. The books can be helpful for reluctant readers by drawing them into an interactive experience that requires strategy and code breaking to solve mysteries.

The series has had success as the combination of learning and gaming are applied using immersive technology. Students around the world are finding a love for reading from the creative

Figure 8.1

Spy Quest is a new augmented reality book series.

approach of *Spy Quest*. The future goals of the company include iBeacon technology to create more location-based gaming elements to coincide with the storyline of the books. The technology will eventually be included with book purchase.

Interactive Stories with Google Spotlight Stories

The Google Spotlight Stories app brings you into the middle of the story. The app can be found in the Google Play and iTunes app store. It contains a handful of virtual reality stories that demonstrate the way stories can now be interactive. Although not all the stories are educational, the concept of virtual reality stories and the progression of storytelling is emphasized in the app.

Each story is a 360° video that can be viewed within the app from every angle. You can view the story within a VR viewer or in full screen mode. When selecting the story, you will begin by downloading the story to your device to easily access it when you open the device again.

While going through the story, the interaction is based on where you are looking. If the story plot is happening in a different location than where the device is pointed, the music fades out and the story is paused. The story resumes when the device is viewing the main plot of the story again. We can provide a more personalized learning experience when our students are given the freedom to explore areas of interest without missing the story.

Some of the stories that can be applied in an elementary classroom are *Windy Day*, *Buggy Night*, and *Duet*. *Windy Day* is about a mouse that struggles to grab a hat on a windy day. As the hat swirls around the scene, you must turn around and look to every angle to continue watching the story. *Buggy Night* is a silly story about a group of bugs that are trying to escape the frog. The story visuals are fantastic as a flashlight captures the interesting sights of insects in the dark. *Duet* is a whimsical love story that is displayed in the sky using hand drawn lines. The story dances around the screen to display this captivating tale.

The app requires a fairly new or powerful device to load the high-quality graphics. If your device is unable to download the app, Google has provided an alternative method of accessing the content by placing nearly all of the stories on YouTube. The difference between the app and the YouTube videos is the interaction. While the app requires the reader to look around to move the story along, the YouTube version simply plays the story as a video.

The combination of immersive technology and storytelling is an exciting opportunity for students to interact with content in new ways. Research is showing that these types of interactions can result in increased empathy and greater engagement with the content. A report from the Tow Center for Digital Journalism shared results from three different types of storytelling: immersive VR (via a head-mounted set), non-immersive VR (desktop-based), and text. The authors found that "stories consumed in VR formats prompted a higher empathetic response than static photo/text treatments and a higher likelihood of participants to take 'political or social action' after viewing (Nieman Lab, 2018)."

As we see the future of storytelling using immersive technology, we'll see more active engagement to modify the results of the story.

Learning Transported Challenge

Explore a story that uses augmented or virtual reality and have students extend the story using Storyfab.

Allow students to demonstrate a story from a book inside of a scene in CoSpaces.

9 Preparing for the Future of Mixed Reality

Many of the immersive technology tools we have today are evolving to offer more engagement, relevance, and simplicity of use. The tools are also improving in how they interact with our world and apply seamlessly to our everyday experiences. With the demonstrated benefits of augmented and virtual reality, immersive technology companies are expanding their involvement in mixed reality.

Changing the Learning Environment with Mixed Reality

The learning environment is changing as immersive technologies continue to grow in the educational market. Our textbooks, devices, and apps are advancing to include many new features. Several companies are on the cutting edge of this field as they release powerful tools for creating immersive experiences.

Lifeliqe

Lifeliqe is one of the pioneering educational companies providing mixed reality content. The company has particularly taken interest in using the Hololens device to display content and interaction through the lens of the device. Wearing the device on your head frees your hands for more interaction. Using your hands, you can navigate through content topics such as the human body, reptiles, and volcanoes. You use gestures within view of the lens that function similar to a mouse control; you can click, resize, and rotate objects using just your hands. Students can now be hands-free to manipulate 3D objects and explore learning as if the object is floating in the classroom.

ARKit

Some of the most recent releases in augmented reality sound very similar to mixed reality. Apple recently announced a developer tool, ARKit, for mobile devices. The tool opens the door for many new features on Apple devices to provide more than a layer of a 3D object. The new features made specifically for Apple apps can identify elements of the physical space, such as walls and tables. We don't need a trigger image for the app to know where to place objects; the technology can now identify the surrounding space to properly and realistically place objects in the correct spot. When a 3D object is placed in a spot, precise tracking will give a realistic experience for the user, who sees the objects in the location and direction oriented to where they are walking. An example of this is Ikea's iOS app, Ikea Place, which allows users to place and move virtual furniture around them in their actual house.

Another new feature is that 3D objects can change color to match the lighting in the physical space. When your device's camera detects a darker area such as a shadow, the augmented reality object is darkened to match the space. The experience will match our real-world view through the camera to give the illusion that the item is actually in our physical environment.

The best ARKit apps released include interactions with design, creation tools, objects interacting with our space, and more. Although the technology is labeled as augmented reality, many of these experiences have the qualities of mixed reality when experienced in a viewer. Because many of the ARKit apps include a transformation of how we interact with content and the way our experience identifies our space, the term mixed reality seems to be a better fit.

Figment

The Figment app creates a way to bring our students on virtual tours by walking through virtual portals. The portals appears as windows to the user. Within the app, portals can easily be dragged into the space you are viewing through your camera and customized with 360° graphics. The person in the experience can walk up to the portal and, when crossing over the space where it was placed, will see the screen change from the camera view into a virtual reality experience. Students can walk through a portal in the classroom that brings them into the middle of a city and then they can walk back out of the portal and into another one that brings them to the beach. These floating windows are viewed through the camera in the app.

Figure 9.1

Using the Figment app, you can create portals into VR worlds.

The option to customize the experience is amazing. The creator can change the 360° experiences by selecting the window and tapping the plus sign in the top of the screen. Select a regular image or a 360° image to load in the window and customize what the experience will include.

Orb

The Orb app brings 3D creation to the next level as you create 3D objects in your space using augmented reality. The app begins by using simple 3D objects such as spheres, cylinders, and rectangular prisms. In the app, the student can add the shape into their reality using the camera. The shapes added in your space can be molded in size and proportion to fit the students' needs. A student can add a cylinder to their space, then stretch it to make it taller. An example of a building project could be the reconstruction of a colonial home or a replica of a war tank. As the students build, they can walk around the structure to modify their object.

Similar to CoSpaces in the virtual world, Orb transforms our physical space using augmented reality. Our students can build anything they can imagine by manipulating 3D objects. This student creation tool is one of the first to use AR to build content that seamlessly works within our physical space. You might have students create monuments for a history project, design worlds with unique ecosystems for science, or bring a literary reference to their reality for a reading assignment. The possibilities are endless!

My Very Hungry Caterpillar AR

Just as the famously hungry caterpillar transforms into a butterfly, our augmented reality apps are morphing into interactive tools. The *Very Hungry Caterpillar* book comes to life in your space, where the caterpillar begins eating and eating and eating until it becomes a butterfly. The caterpillar interacts with your space as you select apples that become food for the insect and your space is transformed to feature the same brilliant colors from the book.

The app is the first of many that will bring books to our world using augmented reality. The app uses the camera to place the caterpillar and stage of props that are included in the book. Following along with the story would be an ideal way to use the app, and considering the future of augmented reality books, we should see the content available explode for our students.

Atlas

Atlas received the biggest "wow" when it was introduced as one of the first ARKit apps. This interactive anatomy app scans the outside and inside of the body. The student can lay the virtual body on a flat surface and walk around the 3D object while it stays in place.

Figure 9.2

Turn the very hungry caterpillar loose in your school garden or cafeteria.

Using your mobile device like a scalpel, you can cut through the body in the gross anatomy lab by moving the device through each part. We can bring our students into the human body by easily navigating our devices through the 3D model.

Within the augmented reality features, students can study human anatomy by removing structures to get a more in-depth view of each part. The app supports seven languages and easily turns any room into a human anatomy lab. The app presents thousands of virtual specimens to explore.

World Brush

The World Brush app was one of the first apps released to draw in space. Similar to the Tilt brush concept on a Vive device, we can now place 3D drawings all around us. Using the various paintbrushes, students can design any object imaginable using their device while walking around their space.

The World Brush has many possibilities to enhance our reality with the addition of customized design. As students begin to design 3D objects for augmented and virtual reality experiences, the goal is to see the content created in World Brush or similar apps and saved and uploaded into other platforms. The ARKit creation apps are fantastic tools to get our students creating content that can be used in other applications.

The ARCore technology by Google provides similar technology to compete with the ARKit in Apple products. As this new technology transforms our mobile devices, we'll see more augmented and mixed reality usage in education. Our use of ARKit and ARCore apps will affect storytelling, building, field trips, exploration, and much more.

Learning Transported Challenge

Build a 3D display of an object from the curriculum you are teaching using augmented or virtual reality. Think of ways your students can create content to add to the creation or develop objects of their own.

Record a video of how your students are using ARKit or ARCore apps to demonstrate knowledge from a lesson. Share it with the #ARVRinEDU community or with your social media followers.

Conclusion

The future of immersive technology is bright as companies invest more money, time, and expertise into entertainment, business, and education. Our students are embracing this technology as quickly as it's released, and our classrooms are quickly gaining options for providing captivating interactive lessons. Immersive technology provides incredible opportunities for personalized learning and enables us to address the needs of all students.

Authentic learning experiences and opportunities that have never been accessible in the classroom are now possible with virtual field trips, interactive stories, and tools that can allow students to explore the world, the solar system, and beyond.

Moving forward, we'll see a transition from providing classroom experiences to giving the creation responsibility to our students. We will see our students take ownership for their learning and design activities that solve the problems that are important to them. Teachers will facilitate a classroom of explorers, developers, and designers as they experience, build, and present their own immersive technology resources.

References

Anomaly (n.d.). Retrieved September 19, 2017 from http://www.experienceanomaly.com/

Augmented Reality. (n.d.). Retrieved from https://www.merriam-webster.com/dictionary/augmented reality

Juan, M., Mendez-Lopez, M., Perez-Hernandez, E., & Albiol-Perez, S. (2014). Augmented Reality for the Assessment of Children's Spatial Memory in Real Settings. PLoSONE, 9(12), e113751. doi:10.1371/journal.pone. 0113751

Mehmet, K., & Yasin, O. (2012). Augmented Reality in Education: Current Technologies and the Potential for Education. Procedia - Social and Behavioral Sciences, 47.

Merge VR. (n.d.). Retrieved from www.dropbox.com/sh/2q0r8rvmcg0y69i/AADq6zHNY_qS9wOfa6ump5Dwa?dl=0

Neiman Labs. (2018). Here's how to make VR content that actually helps users empathize and take action. Retrieved from http://www.niemanlab.org/2018/03/heres-how-to-make-vr-content-that-actually-helps-users-empathize-and-take-action/

Oculus Rift (n.d.). Retrieved from https://www.oculus.com/rift/

Scanlan, C. (2017). Immersive Tech in Education: How xR Plays a Role in Education Today. Retrieved from https://edtechtimes.com/2017/09/22/xr-education-immersive-technology-in-education-today/

Spy Quest. (n.d.). Retrieved from https://twitter.com/SpyQuest

Virtual Reality. (n.d.). Retrieved from https://www.merriam-webster.com/dictionary/virtual reality

Vive Ready Computers (n.d.). Retrieved from https://www.vive.com/us/ready/

Holly, Russell (2016, May 27). "How Much Space Do You Need for your HTC Vive?" VRHeads. Retrieved from https://www.vrheads.com/how-much-space-do-you-need-your-htc-vive

Wikimedia Commons. (2017). No Vale La Pena.jpg. [File]. Retrieved from https://commons.wikimedia.org/w/index.php?title=File:No_Vale_La_Pena.jpg&oldid=242902154.

Appendix A

Immersive Technology App Index

This alphabetical index includes some, not all, of the immersive technology tools mentioned in this book that are available at the time of this writing. Some tools may change and new ones will continue to appear on the scene. In addition to trying out these tools, I encourage you to follow the conversation around AR, VR, and MR tools. A great place to start is the #ARVRinEDu hashtag and Twitter chat.

3DC (3dc.io) 3D modeling app that lets you build, share, and even 3D print your designs. [FREE, iOS, Android and web]

Anomaly (experienceanomaly.com/anomaly/) An interactive AR experience accompanies the science fiction graphic novel Anomaly. The app brings pages of the novel to life. Alternatively, visit ExperienceAnomaly.com/marker to print out a marker and try without the book. [FREE and PAID versions, iOS and Android]

ArCraft Sandbox AR (https://itunes.apple.com/us/app/arcraft-sandbox-ar/id1215001885?mt=8) Augmented reality game that lets you craft and build items with sets of 3D cubes. [FREE, iOS only]

AR Circuits (arcircuits.com) Practice building circuits without an electronics kit. Components can be printed on your home printer and brought to life using a mobile device and augmented reality technology. [PAID]

AR Studio (developers.facebook.com/products/ar-studio/overview) A suite of powerful, customizable tools for AR creators. Create shareable, interactive effects that respond to facial expressions, movements and your surroundings. Place 3D objects in the world and interact with them in real-time. [FREE, iOS]

Aurasma (aurasma.com) App allows you to create trigger images (called auras) and add AR elements and interactive features that will be revealed to viewers using the app. [FREE, iOS, Android]

Blipbuilder (web.blippar.com/blipp-builder) User-friendly augmented reality design tool that allows you to create interactive posters, ads, books and more.

Breakout EDU (breakoutedu.com) Immersive learning games where players use teamwork and critical thinking to solve a series of challenging puzzles in order to open the locked box. Games are available for all ages and content areas. The Breakout EDU Kit costs $150 and includes 12 months of access to the Breakout EDU platform and subject packs containing games developed for a wide variety of curriculums. Access to user-created games and resources is free.

Bubbli (http://bubb.li) Use your smartphone camera to create dynamic spherical photos called bubbles. Add sounds, customize and share your bubbles, or organize them into albums around a theme or event. [FREE]

CoSpaces Education (cospaces.io/edu) This creative online platform, appropriate for all ages and subjects, allows students to create and share 3D and VR experiences. A basic account is free and gives you access to tools, galleries, and Blockly coding tools. A professional version, offering additional scene libraries, assignments and advanced coding tools, starts at $3.50/year per user.

Discovery VR (http://appsload.net/en/apps/89942?utm_campaign=IOSFreeAppUS_discovery-vr&utm_medium=331080520_1155586872801521_89942&utm_source=cpc) Explore immersive video experiences from the Discovery channel, including shows such as Shark Week and Deadliest Catch.

DottyAR (dottyar.com) View and share 3D models online in augmented reality [FREE, iOS, Android]

EON Creator (eonreality.com/platform/eon-creator-avr) Teachers and students can create, experience, and share augmented and virtual reality learning applications and quickly add them to their current classroom.

EON Experience World Builder (tinyurl.com/y7osmfk3) Build, upload, share, and play with AR-created worlds.

Figment AR (viromedia.com/figment) Create imaginative scenes out of the world around you. Add interactive objects to your surroundings, create "portals" to step into another dimension, and add environmental effects like snow, fireworks and more. [FREE, iOS]

Galactic Explorer (spaceplace.nasa.gov/galactic-explorer/en/) Your mission is to safely fly your spacecraft on a journey. You'll want to visit as many galaxies as possible.

Gamar (gamar.com) Create interactive visitor tours in just a few clicks. The Gamar online content management system enables anyone, regardless of their technical skills, to create and manage family trails, educational games and interactive audio tours.

GeoGuessr (geoguessr.com) Web-based graphic discovery game that uses a semi-randomized Google Street View location and requires players to guess their location in the world using only the clues visible.

Google Translate

Google Translate (translate.google.com) The Google Translate "See" feature allows users to see instant translations using their smartphone camera. Over 100 languages available.

Google Earth (earth.google.com) A computer program that renders a 3D representation of Earth based on satellite imagery. Travel to any location in the world, zoom in and see overlays to learn more.

Voyager (tinyurl.com/ydzadbpt) Take interactive tours, learn about science or history.

"I'm Feeling Lucky" Feature Jump to an unknown location in the world.

Streetview (google.com/streetview) Explore landmarks in 360°

Google Spotlight Stories (atap.google.com/spotlight-stories) Immersive, 360° stories that can be experienced through a viewer or on a mobile device.

Human Anatomy Atlas (visiblebody.com/anatomy-and-physiology-apps/human-anatomy-atlas) At $24.99, this app is on the pricey side, but what you get is truly amazing. A comprehensive 3D, AR atlas of the human body. Explore different views and cross sections of the body, reveal definitions and disease descriptions, rotate, zoom and dissect different anatomy regions. This app is so comprehensive it is intended for medical professionals as well as students. [PAID, iOS, Android, Microsoft]

Lifeliqe (lifeliqe.com) Create augmented, virtual and mixed reality experiences in connection with classroom curriculum. Compatible with iOS, Chrome, and Microsoft platforms. District license available for purchase.

Merge Cubes

The future is here! Merge cubes (mergevr.com/cube) are soft foam cubes covered with trigger symbols that reveal 3D experiences when viewed through a smartphone. Imaging holding a lava spewing volcano or human heart in the palm of your hand, turning it to see all angles and allowing multiple viewers to have the same experience. [PAID]

Apps for Merge Cubes

Th!ngs (https://itunes.apple.com/us/app/dig-for-merge-cube/id1253083884?mt=8) This app features holographic mini games that are the perfect way to begin exploring the features of the Merge Cube. [FREE]

Dig It (https://itunes.apple.com/us/app/dig-for-merge-cube/id1253083884?mt=8) allows the user to customize the cube by adding blocks, similar to Minecraft. [FREE]

Metaverse (gometa.io) Platform for creating interactive AR experiences, including games, scavenger hunts, memes, and educational experiences.

MSQRD (msqrd.me) Transform the way you look through amazing masks and effects! Turn into a panda, zombie or even face swap with your friends. Save and share photos and videos, and now broadcast yourself live to your friends, family and fans on Facebook while wearing your favorite masks. [FREE, iOS, Android]

My Very Hungry Caterpillar AR (itunes.apple.com/US/app/id1277085142?mt=8) The caterpillar from the beloved children's story comes to life and crawls around your environment in this interactive app. [PAID, iOS]

Nearpod (nearpod.com) An interactive classroom tool for teachers to engage students with interactive lessons. Free version includes basic features and lesson library. Paid versions include premium features, such as virtual field trips and homework options, as well as options for districts.

Orb (itunes.apple.com/us/app/orb/id1282295219?mt=8) AR building app that allows users to create objects that, when viewed from the device's screen, look like they're in the real world. [FREE, iOS]

Popar Bugs Smart Book (popartoys.com/products/popar-bugs-smart-book) This AR and VR infused hardcover children's book from Popar Toys lets stduents interact with bugs through animations, games, read-alongs, and more! [PAID]

Qlone (qlone.pro) Tool that allows you to scan real objects using your phone's camera, modify them, and export to many 3D file formats, AR & VR experiences, and 3D printers. [FREE, iOS]

QuestUpon (questupon.com) Location-based augmented reality adventures.

Quiver Vision (quivervision.com) Bring your coloring pages to life with augmented reality. [FREE]

RoundMe (roundme.com) Create 360° video experiences. [FREE]

Solar App (aireal.io/producthunt?ref=producthunt) This augmented reality app created by Aerial gives you the ability to walk through and around the entire solar system as if it was part of your real environment. As you're navigating through our planetary system, feel free to tap on a planet to receive detailed information.

Solar System (www.solarsystemscope.com) Experience a 3D representation of the solar system that includes more data on a computer if no mobile devices are available. [FREE]

Spacecraft 3D (tiny.cc/nasaspacecraft) and Android (tiny.cc/nasaandroid) This augmented reality app created by NASA's jet propulsion laboratory allows users to interact with spacecraft, study Earth, and observe the universe. Using a printed AR Target and the camera on your mobile device, you can get up close with these robotic explorers, see how they move, and learn about the engineering feats used to expand our knowledge and understanding of space. [FREE]

Spin Magic (spinmagic.me) [FREE, iOS] Customize your view of the world with this app that features icons, animated stickers, and other AR overlays.

Spy Quest (spy-quest.com) This series of books will immerse children of all ages in the exciting world of international espionage and take them around the world on exciting missions.

Storyfab (story-fab.com) Create augmented reality short films that can be shared.

USA Today VR Stories (usatoday.com/vrstories) Immerse yourself in the stories with the best of our full 360-degree and virtual reality experiences.

Virtual Speech app (virtualspeech.com)

Vuforia Chalk (tiny.cc/chalkapp) This mobile app uses video chats layered with augmented reality to collaborate in real-time. [FREE, iOS]

WallaMe (walla.me) Augmented reality app allows users to hide and share messages in the real world. Take a picture of any surface, write, draw or add stickers and photos, and allow passersby to see your messages. Walls can also be set to private, only available to certain people

World Brush (https://itunes.apple.com/us/app/world-brush/id1277410449?mt=8) AR experience where users can paint with brushes on the world around them. [FREE, iOS]

YouVisit (youvisit.com) Engage audiences through interactive 360° experiences.

Zapworks (zap.works) Robust set of AR content creation tools, including widgets, designer and studio. Create just about any kind of AR experience. [PAID]

Appendix B

ISTE Standards for Students

The ISTE Standards for Students emphasize the skills and qualities we want for students, enabling them to engage and thrive in a connected, digital world. The standards are designed for use by educators across the curriculum, with every age student, with a goal of cultivating these skills throughout a student's academic career. Both students and teachers will be responsible for achieving foundational technology skills to fully apply the standards. The reward, however, will be educators who skillfully mentor and inspire students to amplify learning with technology and challenge them to be agents of their own learning.

1. **Empowered Learner**

   Students leverage technology to take an active role in choosing, achieving and demonstrating competency in their learning goals, informed by the learning sciences. Students:

   a. articulate and set personal learning goals, develop strategies leveraging technology to achieve them and reflect on the learning process itself to improve learning outcomes.

   b. build networks and customize their learning environments in ways that support the learning process.

   c. use technology to seek feedback that informs and improves their practice and to demonstrate their learning in a variety of ways.

   d. understand the fundamental concepts of technology operations, demonstrate the ability to choose, use and troubleshoot current technologies and are able to transfer their knowledge to explore emerging technologies.

2. **Digital Citizen**

   Students recognize the rights, responsibilities and opportunities of living, learning and working in an interconnected digital world, and they act and model in ways that are safe, legal and ethical. Students:

a. cultivate and manage their digital identity and reputation and are aware of the permanence of their actions in the digital world.

b. engage in positive, safe, legal and ethical behavior when using technology, including social interactions online or when using networked devices.

c. demonstrate an understanding of and respect for the rights and obligations of using and sharing intellectual property.

d. manage their personal data to maintain digital privacy and security and are aware of data-collection technology used to track their navigation online.

3. Knowledge Constructor

Students critically curate a variety of resources using digital tools to construct knowledge, produce creative artifacts and make meaningful learning experiences for themselves and others. Students:

a. plan and employ effective research strategies to locate information and other resources for their intellectual or creative pursuits.

b. evaluate the accuracy, perspective, credibility and relevance of information, media, data or other resources.

c. curate information from digital resources using a variety of tools and methods to create collections of artifacts that demonstrate meaningful connections or conclusions.

d. build knowledge by actively exploring real-world issues and problems, developing ideas and theories and pursuing answers and solutions.

4. Innovative Designer

Students use a variety of technologies within a design process to identify and solve problems by creating new, useful or imaginative solutions. Students:

a. know and use a deliberate design process for generating ideas, testing theories, creating innovative artifacts or solving authentic problems.

b. select and use digital tools to plan and manage a design process that considers design constraints and calculated risks.

c. develop, test and refine prototypes as part of a cyclical design process.

d. exhibit a tolerance for ambiguity, perseverance and the capacity to work with open-ended problems.

5. Computational Thinker

Students develop and employ strategies for understanding and solving problems in ways that leverage the power of technological methods to develop and test solutions. Students:

a. formulate problem definitions suited for technology-assisted methods such as data analysis, abstract models and algorithmic thinking in exploring and finding solutions.

b. collect data or identify relevant data sets, use digital tools to analyze them, and represent data in various ways to facilitate problem-solving and decision-making.

c. break problems into component parts, extract key information, and develop descriptive models to understand complex systems or facilitate problem-solving.

d. understand how automation works and use algorithmic thinking to develop a sequence of steps to create and test automated solutions.

6. Creative Communicator

Students communicate clearly and express themselves creatively for a variety of purposes using the platforms, tools, styles, formats and digital media appropriate to their goals. Students:

a. choose the appropriate platforms and tools for meeting the desired objectives of their creation or communication.

b. create original works or responsibly repurpose or remix digital resources into new creations.

c. communicate complex ideas clearly and effectively by creating or using a variety of digital objects such as visualizations, models or simulations.

d. publish or present content that customizes the message and medium for their intended audiences.

7. Global Collaborator

Students use digital tools to broaden their perspectives and enrich their learning by collaborating with others and working effectively in teams locally and globally. Students:

a. use digital tools to connect with learners from a variety of backgrounds and cultures, engaging with them in ways that broaden mutual understanding and learning.

b. use collaborative technologies to work with others, including peers, experts or community members, to examine issues and problems from multiple viewpoints.

c. contribute constructively to project teams, assuming various roles and responsibilities to work effectively toward a common goal.

d. explore local and global issues and use collaborative technologies to work with others to investigate solutions.